Extreme Programming
Explained

Extreme Programming
Explained

Embrace Change

Kent Beck

ADDISON-WESLEY

An imprint of Addison Wesley Longman, Inc.

Reading, Massachusetts • Harlow, England • Menlo Park, California
Berkeley, California • Don Mills, Ontario • Sydney
Bonn • Amsterdam • Tokyo • Mexico City

The publisher offers discounts on this book when ordered in quantity for special sales. For more information, please contact:

Corporate, Government, and Special Sales Group
Addison Wesley Longman, Inc.
One Jacob Way
Reading, Massachusetts 01867

Library of Congress Cataloging-in-Publication Data

Beck, Kent.
    Extreme programming explained: embrace change / Kent Beck.
        p. cm.
    ISBN 201-61641-6 (alk. paper)
    1. Computer software--Development.   2. Extreme programming
I. Title.
    QA76.76.D47B434 1999   99-36995
    005.1--dc21   CIP

Text printed on recycled and acid-free paper.

2 3 4 5 6 7 8 9 – CRS – 03 02 01 00 99
Second printing, November 1999

To Dad

Thanks to Cindee Andres, my wife and partner, for insisting that I ignore her and write. Thanks to Bethany, Lincoln, Lindsey, Forrest, and Joelle for giving up time with me so I could type.

Contents

Foreword

Extreme Programming (XP) nominates coding as the key activity throughout a software project. This can't possibly work!

Time to reflect for a second about my own development work. I work in a just-in-time software culture with compressed release cycles spiced up with high technical risk. Having to make change your friend is a survival skill. Communication in and across often geographically separated teams is done with code. We read code to understand new or evolving subsystem APIs. The life cycle and behavior of complex objects is defined in test cases, again in code. Problem reports come with test cases demonstrating the problem, once more in code. Finally, we continuously improve existing code with refactoring. Obviously our development is code-centric, but we successfully deliver software in time, so this can work after all.

It would be wrong to conclude that all that is needed to deliver software is daredevil programming. Delivering software is hard, and delivering quality software in time is even harder. To make it work requires the disciplined use of additional best practices. This is where Kent starts in his thought-provoking book on XP.

Kent was among the leaders at Tektronics to recognize the potential of man in the loop pair programming in Smalltalk for complex engineering applications. Together with Ward Cunningham, he inspired much of the pattern movement that has had such an impact on my career. XP describes an approach to development that combines practices used by many successful developers that got buried under the massive literature on software methods and process. Like patterns, XP builds on best practices such as unit testing, pair programming, and refactoring. In XP these practices are combined so that they complement and often control each other. The focus is on the interplay of the different practices, which makes this book an important contribution. There is a single goal to deliver software with the right functionality and hitting dates. While OTI's successful Just In Time Software process is not pure XP, it has many common threads.

I've enjoyed my interaction with Kent and practicing XP episodes on a little thing called Junit. His views and approaches always challenge the way I approach software development. There is no doubt that XP challenges some traditional big M approaches; this book will let you decide whether you want to embrace XP or not.

Erich Gamma

Preface

This is a book about Extreme Programming (XP). XP is a light-weight methodology for small-to-medium-sized teams developing software in the face of vague or rapidly changing requirements. This book is intended to help you decide if XP is for you.

To some folks, XP seems like just good common sense. So why the "extreme" in the name? XP takes commonsense principles and practices to extreme levels.

- ⟡ If code reviews are good, we'll review code all the time (pair programming).
- ⟡ If testing is good, everybody will test all the time (unit testing), even the customers (functional testing).
- ⟡ If design is good, we'll make it part of everybody's daily business (refactoring).
- ⟡ If simplicity is good, we'll always leave the system with the simplest design that supports its current functionality (the simplest thing that could possibly work).
- ⟡ If architecture is important, everybody will work defining and refining the architecture all the time (metaphor).
- ⟡ If integration testing is important, then we'll integrate and test several times a day (continuous integration).
- ⟡ If short iterations are good, we'll make the iterations really, really short—seconds and minutes and hours, not weeks and months and years (the Planning Game).

When I first articulated XP, I had the mental image of knobs on a control board. Each knob was a practice that from experience I knew worked well. I would turn all the knobs up to 10 and see what happened. I was a little surprised to find that the whole package of practices was stable, predictable, and flexible.

XP makes two sets of promises.

◇ To programmers, XP promises that they will be able to work on things that really matter, every day. They won't have to face scary situations alone. They will be able to do everything in their power to make their system successful. They will make decisions that they can make best, and they won't make decisions they they aren't best qualified to make.

◇ To customers and managers, XP promises that they will get the most possible value out of every programming week. Every few weeks they will be able to see concrete progress on goals they care about. They will be able to change the direction of the project in the middle of development without incurring exorbitant costs.

In short, XP promises to reduce project risk, improve responsiveness to business changes, improve productivity throughout the life of a system, and add fun to building software in teams—all at the same time. Really. Quit laughing. Now you'll have to read the rest of the book to see if I'm crazy.

This Book

This book talks about the thinking behind XP—its roots, philosophy, stories, myths. It is intended to help you make an informed decision about whether or not to use XP on your project. If you read this book and correctly decide *not* to use XP for your project, I will have met my goal just as much as if you correctly decide *to* use it. A second goal of this book is to help those of you already using XP to understand it better.

This isn't a book about precisely how to do Extreme Programming. You won't read lots of checklists here, or see many examples, or lots of programming stories. For that, you will have to go online, talk to some of the coaches mentioned here, wait for the topical, how-to books to follow, or just make up your own version.

The next stage of acceptance of XP is now in the hands of a group of people (you may be one) who are dissatisfied with software development as it is currently practiced. You want a better way to develop software, you want better relationships with your customers, you want happier, more stable, more productive programmers. In short, you are looking for big rewards, and you aren't afraid to try new ideas to get them. But if you are going to take a risk, you want to be convinced that you aren't just being stupid.

XP tells you to do things differently. Sometimes XP's advice is absolutely contrary to accepted wisdom. Right now I expect those choosing to use XP to require compelling reasons for doing things differently, but if the reasons are there, to go right ahead. I wrote this book to give you those reasons.

What Is XP?

What is XP? XP is a lightweight, efficient, low-risk, flexible, predictable, scientific, and fun way to develop software. It is distinguished from other methodologies by

- ◇ Its early, concrete, and continuing feedback from short cycles.
- ◇ Its incremental planning approach, which quickly comes up with an overall plan that is expected to evolve through the life of the project.
- ◇ Its ability to flexibly schedule the implementation of functionality, responding to changing business needs.
- ◇ Its reliance on automated tests written by programmers and customers to monitor the progress of development, to allow the system to evolve, and to catch defects early.
- ◇ Its reliance on oral communication, tests, and source code to communicate system structure and intent.
- ◇ Its reliance on an evolutionary design process that lasts as long as the system lasts.

- ✧ Its reliance on the close collaboration of programmers with ordinary skills.
- ✧ Its reliance on practices that work with both the short-term instincts of programmers and the long-term interests of the project.

XP is a discipline of software development. It is a discipline because there are certain things that you have to do to be doing XP. You don't get to choose whether or not you will write tests—if you don't, you aren't extreme: end of discussion.

XP is designed to work with projects that can be built by teams of two to ten programmers, that aren't sharply constrained by the existing computing environment, and where a reasonable job of executing tests can be done in a fraction of a day.

XP frightens or angers some people who encounter it for the first time. However, none of the ideas in XP are new. Most are as old as programming. There is a sense in which XP is conservative—all its techniques have been proven over decades (for the implementation strategy) or centuries (for the management strategy).

The innovation of XP is

- ✧ Putting all these practices under one umbrella.
- ✧ Making sure they are practiced as thoroughly as possible.
- ✧ Making sure the practices support each other to the greatest possible degree.

Enough

In *The Forest People* and *The Mountain People*, anthropologist Colin Turnbull paints contrasting pictures of two societies. In the mountains, resources were scarce and people were always on the brink of starvation. The culture they evolved was horrific. Mothers abandoned babies to roving packs of feral children as soon as they had any chance of survival. Violence, brutality, and betrayal were the order of the day.

In contrast, the forest had plenty of resources. A person had only to spend half an hour a day providing for their basic needs. The forest culture was the mirror image of the mountain culture. Adults shared in raising children, who were nurtured and loved until they were quite ready to care for themselves. If one person accidentally killed another (deliberate crime was unknown), they were exiled, but they only had to go a little ways into the forest, and only for a few months, and even then the other tribespeople brought them gifts of food.

XP is an experiment in answer to the question, "How would you program if you had enough time?" Now, you can't have extra time, because this is business after all, and we are certainly playing to win. But if you had enough time, you would write tests; you would restructure the system when you learned something; you would talk a lot with fellow programmers and with the customer.

Such a "mentality of sufficiency" is humane, unlike the relentless drudgery of impossible, imposed deadlines that drives so much talent out of the business of programming. The mentality of sufficiency is also good business. It creates its own efficiencies, just as the mentality of scarcity creates its own waste.

Outline

The book is written as if you and I were creating a new software development discipline together. We start by examining our basic assumptions about software development. We then create the discipline itself. We conclude by examing the implications of what we have created—how it can be adopted, when it shouldn't be adopted, and what opportunities it creates for business.

The book is divided into three sections.

- ✧ The Problem—The chapters from "Risk: The Basic Problem" to "Back to Basics" set up the problem Extreme Programming is trying to solve and present criteria for evaluating the solution. This section will give you an idea of the overall worldview of Extreme Programming.
- ✧ The Solution—The chapters from "Quick Overview" to "Testing Strategy" turn the abstract ideas in the first section into the practices of a concrete methodology. This section will not tell you exactly how you can execute the practices, but rather talks about

their general shape. The discussion of each practice relates it to the problems and principles introduced in the first section.

⋄ Implementing XP—The chapters from "Adopting XP" to "XP at Work" describe a variety of topics around implementing XP—how to adopt it, what is expected from the various people in an extreme project, how XP looks to the business folks.

Acknowledgments

I write in the first person here, not because these are my ideas, but rather because this is my perspective on these ideas. Most of the practices in XP are as old as programming.

Ward Cunningham is my immediate source for much of what you will read here. In many ways I have spent the last fifteen years just trying to explain to other people what he does naturally. Thanks to Ron Jeffries for trying it, then making it much better. Thanks to Martin Fowler for explaining it in a nonthreatening way. Thanks to Erich Gamma for long talks while watching the swans in the Limmat, and for not letting me get away with sloppy thinking. And none of this would have happened if I hadn't watched my dad, Doug Beck, ply his programming craft all those years.

Thanks to the C3 team at Chrysler for following me up the hill, then storming past me on the way to the top. And special thanks to our managers Sue Unger and Ron Savage for the courage to give us the chance to try.

Thanks to Daedalos Consulting for supporting the writing of this book.

Champion reviewer honors go to Paul Chisolm for his copious, thoughtful, and often downright annoying comments. This book wouldn't be half of what it is without his feedback.

I have really enjoyed my interactions with all my reviewers. Well, at least I have gained tremendous help from them. I can't thank them enough for wading through my 1.0 prose, some of them in a foreign language. Thanks to (listed in the random order in which I read their reviews) Greg Hutchinson, Massimo Arnoldi, Dave Cleal, Sames Schuster, Don Wells, Joshua Kerievsky, Thorsten Dittmar, Moritz Becker, Daniel Gubler, Christoph Henrici, Thomas Zang, Dierk

Koenig, Miroslav Novak, Rodney Ryan, Frank Westphal, Paul Trunz, Steve Hayes, Kevin Bradtke, Jeanine De Guzman, Tom Kubit, Falk Bruegmann, Hasko Heinecke, Peter Merel, Rob Mee, Pete McBreen, Thomas Ernst, Guido Haechler, Dieter Holz, Martin Knecht, Dierk König, Dirk Krampe, Patrick Lisser, Elisabeth Maier, Thomas Mancini, Alexio Moreno, Rolf Pfenninger, and Matthias Ressel.

Section 1

The Problem

This section sets the stage for Extreme Programming by discussing various aspects of the problem to be solved in inventing a new discipline of software development. The section discusses the basic assumptions we will use as we choose practices covering the various aspects of software development—the driving metaphor, the four values, the principles derived from those values, and the activities to be structured by our new development discipline.

Chapter 1

Risk: The Basic Problem

Software development fails to deliver, and fails to deliver value.
This failure has huge economic and human impact. We need to
find a new way to develop software.

The basic problem of software development is risk. Here are some examples of risk:

- Schedule slips—the day for delivery comes, and you have to tell the customer that the software won't be ready for another six months.
- Project canceled—after numerous slips, the project is canceled without ever going into production.
- System goes sour—the software is successfully put into production, but after a couple of years the cost of making changes or the defect rate rises so much that the system must be replaced.
- Defect rate—the software is put into production, but the defect rate is so high that it isn't used.
- Business misunderstood—the software is put into production, but it doesn't solve the business problem that was originally posed.
- Business changes—the software is put into production, but the business problem it was designed to solve was replaced six months ago by another, more pressing, business problem.
- False feature rich—the software has a host of potentially interesting features, all of which were fun to program, but none of which makes the customer much money.

✧ Staff turnover—after two years, all the good programmers on the project begin to hate the program and leave.

In these pages you will read about Extreme Programming (XP), a software development discipline that addresses risk at all levels of the development process. XP is also very productive, produces high-quality software, and is a lot of fun to execute.

How does XP address the risks listed above?

✧ Schedule slips—XP calls for short release cycles, a few months at most, so the scope of any slip is limited. Within a release, XP uses one- to four-week iterations of customer-requested features for fine-grained feedback about progress. Within an iteration, XP plans with one- to three-day tasks, so the team can solve problems even during an iteration. Finally, XP calls for implementing the highest priority features first, so any features that slip past the release will be of lower value.

✧ Project canceled—XP asks the customer to choose the smallest release that makes the most business sense, so there is less to go wrong before going into production and the value of the software is greatest.

✧ System goes sour—XP creates and maintains a comprehensive suite of tests, which are run and re-run after every change (several times a day), to ensure a quality baseline. XP always keeps the system in prime condition. Cruft is not allowed to accumulate.

✧ Defect rate—XP tests from the perspective of both programmers writing tests function-by-function and customers writing tests program-feature-by-program-feature.

✧ Business misunderstood—XP calls for the customer to be an integral part of the team. The specification of the project is continuously refined during development, so learning by the customer and the team can be reflected in the software.

✧ Business changes—XP shortens the release cycle, so there is less change during the development of a single release. During a release, the customer is welcome to substitute new functionality for functionality not yet completed. The team doesn't even notice if it is working on newly discovered functionality or features defined years ago.

✧ False feature rich—XP insists that only the highest priority tasks are addressed.

✧ Staff turnover—XP asks programmers to accept responsibility for estimating and completing their own work, gives them feedback about the actual time taken so their estimates can improve, and respects those estimates. The rules for who can make and change estimates are clear. Thus, there is less chance for a programmer to get frustrated by being asked to do the obviously impossible. XP also encourages human contact among the team, reducing the loneliness that is often at the heart of job dissatisfaction. Finally, XP incorporates an explicit model of staff turnover. New team members are encouraged to gradually accept more and more responsibility, and are assisted along the way by each other and by existing programmers.

Our Mission

If we accept project risk as the problem to be solved, where are we going to look for the solution? What we need to do is invent a style of software development that addresses these risks. We need to communicate this discipline as clearly as possible to programmers, managers, and customers. We need to set out guidelines for adapting it to local conditions (that is, communicate what is fixed and what is variable).

That's what we cover in sections one and two of this book. We will go step by step through the aspects of the problem of creating a new style or discipline of development, and then we will solve the problem. From a set of basic assumptions, we will derive solutions that dictate how the various activities in software development—planning, testing, development, design, and deployment—should occur.

Chapter 2

A Development Episode

Day-to-day programming proceeds from a task clearly connected to a feature the customer wants, to tests, to implementation, to design, and through to integration. A little of each of the activities of software development are packed into each episode.

But first a little peek ahead to where we are going. This chapter is the story of the heartbeat of XP—the development episode. This is where a programmer implements an engineering task (the smallest unit of scheduling) and integrates it with the rest of the system.

I look at my stack of task cards. The top one says "Export Quarter-to-date Withholding." At this morning's stand-up meeting, I remember you said you had finished the quarter-to-date calculation. I ask if you (my hypothetical teammate) have time to help with the export. "Sure," you say. The rule is, if you're asked for help you have to say "yes." We have just become pair programming partners.

We spend a couple of minutes discussing the work you did yesterday. You talk about the bins you added, what the tests are like, maybe a little about how you noticed yesterday that pair programming worked better when you moved the monitor back a foot.

You ask, "What are the test cases for this task?"

I say, "When we run the export station, the values in the export record should match the values in the bins."

"Which fields have to be populated?" you ask.

"I don't know. Let's ask Eddie."

We interrupt Eddie for 30 seconds. He explains the five fields that he knows about that are related to quarter-to-date.

We go look at the structure of some of the existing export test cases. We find one that is almost what we need. By abstracting a superclass, we can implement our test case easily. We do the refactoring. We run the existing tests. They all run.

We notice that several other export test cases could take advantage of the superclass we just created. We want to see some results on the task, so we just write down "Retrofit AbstractExportTest" on our to-do card.

Now we write the test case. Since we just made the test case super-class, writing the new test case is easy. We are done in a few minutes. About halfway through, I say, "I can even see how we will implement this. We can …"

"Let's get the test case finished first," you interrupt. While we're writing the test case, ideas for three variations come to mind. You write them on the to-do card.

We finish the test case and run it. It fails. Naturally. We haven't implemented anything yet. "Wait a minute," you say. "Yesterday, Ralph and I were working on a calculator in the morning. We wrote five test cases that we thought would break. All but one of them ran first thing."

We bring up a debugger on the test case. We look at the objects we have to compute with.

I write the code. (Or you do, whoever has the clearest idea.) While we are implementing, we notice a couple more test cases we should write. We put them on the to-do card. The test case runs.

We go to the next test case, and the next. I implement them. You notice that the code could be made simpler. You try to explain to me how to simplify. I get frustrated trying to listen to you and implement at the same time, so I push the keyboard over to you. You refactor the code. You run the test cases. They pass. You implement the next couple of test cases.

After a while, we look at the to-do card and the only item on it is restructuring the other test cases. Things have gone smoothly, so we go ahead and restructure them, making sure they run when we finish.

Now the to-do list is empty. We notice that the integration machine is free. We load the latest release. Then we load our changes. Then we run all the test cases, our new ones and all the tests everyone else has ever written. One fails. "That's strange. It's been almost a month since I've had a test case break during integration," you say. No problem. We debug the test case and fix the code. Then we run the whole suite again. This time it passes. We release our code.

That's the whole XP development cycle. Notice that:

- Pairs of programmers program together.
- Development is driven by tests. You test first, then code. Until all the tests run, you aren't done. When all the tests run, and you can't think of any more tests that would break, you are done adding functionality.
- Pairs don't just make test cases run. They also evolve the design of the system. Changes aren't restricted to any particular area. Pairs add value to the analysis, design, implementation, and testing of the system. They add that value wherever the system needs it.
- Integration immediately follows development, including integration testing.

Chapter 3

Economics of Software Development

We need to make our software development economically more valuable by spending money more slowly, earning revenue more quickly, and increasing the probable productive lifespan of our project. But most of all we need to increase the options for business decisions.[1]

By adding up the cash flows in and out of the project, we can simply analyze what makes a software project valuable. By taking into account the effect of interest rates, we can calculate the net present value of the cash flows. We can further refine our analysis by multiplying the discounted cash flows by the probability that the project will survive to pay or earn those cash flows.

With these three factors—

⋄ Cash flows in and out
⋄ Interest rates
⋄ Project mortality

we can create a strategy for maximizing the economic value of the project. We can do this by

⋄ Spending less, which is difficult because everyone starts off with pretty much the same tools and skills.

---

1. Thanks to John Favaro for the analysis of XP with options pricing.

- ◇ Earning more, which is only possible with a superior marketing and sales organization, not topics we will cover in this book (thank goodness).
- ◇ Spending later and earning sooner, so we pay less interest on the money we spend and we earn more interest on the money we receive.
- ◇ Increasing the probability that the project will stay alive, so we are more likely to get the big payoff late in the project.

Options

There is another way of looking at the economics of a software project—as a series of options. Software project management can be looked at as having four kinds of options:

- ◇ Option to abandon—you can get something out of the project even if you cancel it. The more value you can take from the project without actually delivering it in its originally envisioned form, the better.
- ◇ Option to switch—you can change the direction of a project. A project management strategy is more valuable if halfway through a project the customers can change the requirements. The more often and the more violently the requirements can change, the better.
- ◇ Option to defer—you can wait until the situation has sorted itself out before investing. A project management strategy is more valuable if you can wait to spend money without completely losing the opportunity to invest. The longer the deferral and the more money that can be deferred, the better.
- ◇ Option to grow—if a market looks to be taking off, you can grow quickly to take advantage of it. A project management strategy is more valuable if it can gracefully scale up to greater and greater production given greater investment. The faster and longer the project can grow, the better.

Calculating the worth of options is two parts art, five parts mathematics, and one part good old-fashioned Kentucky windage.

There are five factors involved:

- ✧ The amount of investment required to get the option
- ✧ The price at which you can purchase the prize if you exercise the option
- ✧ The current value of the prize
- ✧ The amount of time in which you can exercise the options
- ✧ The uncertainty in the eventual value of the prize

Of these, the worth of options is generally dominated by the last factor, the uncertainty. From this we can make a concrete prediction. Suppose we create a project management strategy that maximizes the value of the project analyzed as options by providing

- ✧ Accurate and frequent feedback about progress
- ✧ Many opportunities to dramatically change the requirements
- ✧ A smaller initial investment
- ✧ The opportunity to go faster

The greater the uncertainty, the more valuable the strategy will become. This is true whether the uncertainty comes from technical risk, a changing business environment, or rapidly evolving requirements. (This provides a theoretical answer to the question, "When should I use XP?" Use XP when requirements are vague or changing.)

Example

Suppose you're programming merrily along and you see that you could add a feature that would cost you $10. You figure the return on this feature (its net present value) is somewhere around $15. So the net present value of adding this feature is $5.

Suppose you knew in your heart that it wasn't clear at all how much this new feature would be worth—it was just your guess, not something you really knew was worth $15 to the customer. In fact, you figure that its value to the customer could vary as much as 100% from your estimate. Suppose further (see Chapter 5, Cost of Change, page 21) that it would still cost you about $10 to add that feature one year from now.

What would be the value of the strategy of just waiting, of not implementing the feature now? Well, at the usual interest rates of about 5%, the options theory calculator cranks out a value of $7.87.

The option of waiting is worth *more* than the value (NPV = $5) of investing *now* to add the feature. Why? With that much uncertainty, the feature certainly might be much more valuable to the customer, in which case you're no worse off waiting than you would have been by implementing it now. Or it could be worth zilch—in which case you've saved the trouble of a worthless exercise.

In the jargon of trading, options "eliminate downside risk."

Chapter 4

Four Variables

We will control four variables in our projects—cost, time, quality, and scope. Of these, scope provides us the most valuable form of control.

Here is a model of software development from the perspective of a system of control variables. In this model, there are four variables in software development:

- ✧ Cost
- ✧ Time
- ✧ Quality
- ✧ Scope

The way the software development game is played in this model is that external forces (customers, managers) get to pick the values of any three of the variables. The development team gets to pick the resultant value of the fourth variable.

Some managers and customers believe they can pick the value of all four variables. "You are *going* to get all these requirements done by the first of next month with exactly this team. And quality is job one here, so it will be up to our usual standards." When this happens, quality always goes out the window (this is generally up to the usual standards, though), since nobody does good work under too much stress. Also likely to go out of control is time. You get crappy software late.

The solution is to make the four variables visible. If everyone—programmers, customers, and managers—can see all four variables, they can consciously choose which variables to control. If they don't like the result implied for the fourth variable, they can change the inputs, or they can pick a different three variables to control.

Interactions Between the Variables

Cost—More money can grease the skids a little, but too much money too soon creates more problems than it solves. On the other hand, give a project too little money and it won't be able to solve the customer's business problem.

Time—More time to deliver can improve quality and increase scope. Since feedback from systems in production is vastly higher quality than any other kind of feedback, giving a project too much time will hurt it. Give a project too little time and quality suffers, with scope, time, and cost not far behind.

Quality—Quality is terrible as a control variable. You can make very short-term gains (days or weeks) by deliberately sacrificing quality, but the cost—human, business, and technical—is enormous.

Scope—Less scope makes it possible to deliver better quality (as long as the customer's business problem is still solved). It also lets you deliver sooner or cheaper.

There is not a simple relationship between the four variables. For example, you can't just get software faster by spending more money. As the saying goes, "Nine women cannot make a baby in one month." (And contrary to what I've heard from some managers, eighteen women still can't make a baby in one month.)

In many ways, cost is the most constrained variable. You can't just spend your way to quality, or scope, or short release cycles. In fact, at the beginning of a project, you can't spend much at all. The investment has to start small and grow over time. After a while, you can productively spend more and more money.

I had one client who said, "We have promised to deliver all of this functionality. To do that, we have to have 40 programmers."

I said, "You can't have 40 programmers on the first day. You have to start with one team. Then grow to two. Then four. In two years you can have 40 programmers, but not today."

They said, "You don't understand. We have to have 40 programmers." I said, "You can't have 40 programmers." They said, "We have to."

They didn't. I mean, they did. They hired the 40 programmers. Things didn't go well. The programmers left; they hired 40 more. Four years later they are just beginning to deliver value to the business, one small subproject at a time, and they nearly got canceled first.

All the constraints on cost can drive managers crazy. Especially if they are focused on an annual budgeting process, they are so used to driving everything from cost that they will make big mistakes ignoring the constraints on how much control cost gives you.

The other problem with cost is that higher costs often feed tangential goals, like status or prestige. "Of course, I have a project with 150 people (sniff, sniff)." This can lead to projects that fail because the manager wanted to look impressive. After all, how much status is there in staffing the same project with 10 programmers and delivering in half the time?

On the other hand, cost is deeply related to the other variables. Within the range of investment that can sensibly be made, by spending more money you can increase the scope, or you can move more deliberately and increase quality, or you can (to some extent) reduce time to market.

Spending money can also reduce friction—faster machines, more technical specialists, better offices.

The constraints on controlling projects by controlling time generally come from outside—the year 2000 being the most recent example. The end of the year; before the quarter starts; when the old system is scheduled to be shut off; a big trade show—these are some examples of external time constraints. So, the time variable is often out of the hands of the project manager and in the hands of the customer.

Quality is another strange variable. Often, by insisting on better quality you can get projects done sooner, or you can get more done in a given amount of time. This happened to me when I started writing unit tests (as described in Chapter 2, A Development Episode, page 7). As soon as I had my tests, I had so much more confidence in my code that I wrote faster, without stress. I could clean up my system more easily, which made further development easier. I've also seen this happen with teams. As soon as they start testing, or as soon as they agree on coding standards, they start going faster.

There is a strange relationship between internal and external quality. External quality is quality as measured by the customer. Internal quality is quality as measured by the programmers. Temporarily sacrificing internal quality to reduce time to market in hopes that external quality won't suffer too much is a tempting short-term play. And you can often get away with making a mess for a matter of weeks or months. Eventually, though, internal quality problems will catch up with you and make your software prohibitively expensive to maintain, or unable to reach a competitive level of external quality.

On the other hand, from time to time you can get done sooner by relaxing quality constraints. Once, I was working on a system to plug replace a legacy COBOL system. Our quality constraint was that we precisely reproduce the answers produced by the old system. As we got closer and closer to our release date, it became apparent that we could reproduce all the errors in the old system, but only by shipping much later. We went to the customers, showed them that our answers were more correct, and offered them the option of shipping on time if they wanted to believe our answers instead.

There is a human effect from quality. Everybody wants to do a good job, and they work much better if they feel they are doing good work. If you deliberately downgrade quality, your team might go faster at first, but soon the demoralization of producing crap will overwhelm any gains you temporarily made from not testing, or not reviewing, or not sticking to standards.

Focus on Scope

Lots of people know about cost, quality, and time as control variables, but don't acknowledge the fourth. For software development, scope is the most important variable to be aware of. Neither the programmers nor the business people have more than a vague idea about what is valuable about the software under development. One of the most powerful decisions in project management is eliminating scope. If you actively manage scope, you can provide managers and customers with control over cost, quality, and time.

One of the great things about scope is that it is a variable that varies a lot. For decades, programmers have been whining, "The customers can't tell us what they want. When we give them what they say they want, they don't like it." This is an absolute truth of software development. The requirements are never clear at first. Customers can never tell you exactly what they want.

The development of a piece of software changes its own requirements. As soon as the customers see the first release, they learn what they want in the second release...or what they really wanted in the first. And it's valuable learning, because it couldn't have possibly taken place based on speculation. It is learning that can only come from experience. But customers can't get there alone. They need people who can program, not as guides, but as companions.

What if we see the "softness" of requirements as an opportunity, not a problem? Then we can choose to see scope as the easiest of the four variables to control. Because it is so soft, we can shape it—a little this way, a little that way. If time gets tight toward a release date, there is always something that can be deferred to the next release. By not trying to do too much, we preserve our ability to produce the required quality on time.

If we created a discipline of development based on this model, we would fix the date, quality, and cost of a piece of software. We would look at the scope implied by the first three variables. Then, as development progressed, we would continually adjust the scope to match conditions as we found them.

This would have to be a process that tolerated change easily, because the project would change direction often. You wouldn't want to spend a lot on software that turned out not to be used. You wouldn't want to build a road you never drove on because you took another turn. Also, you would have to have a process that kept the cost of changes reasonable for the life of the system.

If you dropped important functionality at the end of every release cycle, the customer would soon get upset. To avoid this, XP uses two strategies:

1. You get lots of practice making estimates and feeding back the actual results. Better estimates reduce the probability that you will have to drop functionality.
2. You implement the customer's most important requirements first, so if further functionality has to be dropped it is less important than the functionality that is already running in the system.

Chapter 5

Cost of Change

Under certain circumstances, the exponential rise in the cost of changing software over time can be flattened. If we can flatten the curve, old assumptions about the best way to develop software no longer hold.

One of the universal assumptions of software engineering is that the cost of changing a program rises exponentially over time. I can remember sitting in a big linoleum-floored classroom as a college junior and seeing the professor draw on the board the curve found in Figure 1.

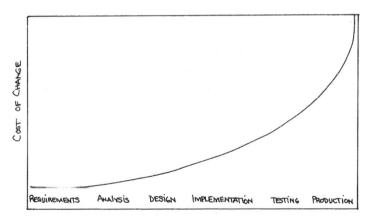

FIGURE 1. **The cost of change rising exponentially over time**

"The cost to fix a problem in a piece of software rises exponentially over time. A problem that might take a dollar to fix if you found it during requirements analysis might costs thousands to fix once the software is in production."

I resolved then and there that I would never let a problem get through to production. No sirree, I was going to catch problems as soon as possible. I would work out every possible problem in advance. I would review and crosscheck my code. No way was I going to cost my employer $100,000.

The problem is that this curve is no longer valid. Or rather, with a combination of technology and programming practices, it is possible to experience a curve that is really quite the opposite. Now stories are possible like the following, which happened to me recently on a life insurance contract management system:

1700—I discover that as near as I can tell, the fabulous feature of our system where a single transaction can have debits from several accounts and credits to several accounts simply isn't used. Each transaction comes from one account and goes to one other. Is it possible to simplify the system as in Figure 2?

1702—I ask Massimo to come sit with me while we examine the situation. We write a query. Out of the 300,000 transactions in the system, every single one of them has a single debit and a single credit account.

1705—If we were going to fix the mistake, how would we do it? We would change the interface of the Transaction and change the implementation. We write the required four methods and start the tests.

1715—The tests (more than 1,000 unit and functional tests) still run 100%. We can't think of any reason the changes won't work. We start working on the database migration code.

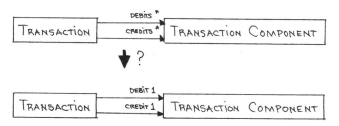

FIGURE 2. **Can we have a single component each for debit and credit?**

1720—The nightly batches are finished and the database has been backed up. We install the new versions of the code and run the migration.

1730—We run a few sanity tests. Everything we can think of works. Unable to think of anything else to do, we go home.

The next day—The error logs are clear. No complaints from the users. The change worked.

Over the next couple of weeks we discovered a series of further simplifications enabled by the new structure that allow us to open up the accounting part of the system to entirely new functionality, all the while making the system simpler, clearer, and less redundant.

The software development community has spent enormous resources in recent decades trying to reduce the cost of change—better languages, better database technology, better programming practices, better environments and tools, new notations.

What would we do if all that investment paid off? What if all that work on languages and databases and whatnot actually got somewhere? What if the cost of change didn't rise exponentially over time, but rose much more slowly, eventually reaching an asymptote? What if tomorrow's software engineering professor draws Figure 3 on the board?

This is one of the premises of XP. It is *the* technical premise of XP. If the cost of change rose slowly over time, you would act completely differently from how you do under the assumption that costs rise exponentially. You would make big decisions as late in the process as possible, to

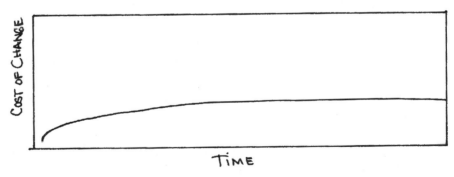

FIGURE 3. **The cost of change may not rise dramatically over time**

defer the cost of making the decisions and to have the greatest possible chance that they would be right. You would only implement what you had to, in hopes that the needs you anticipate for tomorrow wouldn't come true. You would introduce elements to the design only as they simplified existing code or made writing the next bit of code simpler.

If a flattened change cost curve makes XP possible, a steep change cost curve makes XP impossible. If change is ruinously expensive, you would be crazy to charge ahead without careful forethought. But if change stays cheap, the additional value and reduced risk of early concrete feedback outweighs the additional cost of early change.

Keeping the cost of change low doesn't just happen magically. There are technologies and practices that keep software pliable.

On the technology side, objects are a key technology. Message sending is a powerful way to cheaply build many opportunities for change. Each message becomes a potential point for future modification, a modification that can take place without touching the existing code.

Object databases transfer this flexibility into the realm of permanent storage. With an object database, it is possible to migrate objects in one format into objects in another format easily, since the code is attached to the data, not separated as in earlier database technologies. Even if you can't find a way to migrate the objects, you can have two alternative implementations coexisting.

This is not to say that you must have objects to have flexibility. I learned the fundamentals of XP by watching my dad write real-time process control code in assembler. He developed a style that made it possible for him to continuously refine the design of his programs. However, my experience is that the cost of change rises more steeply without objects than with objects.

This is not to say that objects are enough. I have seen (and probably written, if truth be known) loads of object-oriented code that no one wanted to touch.

Several factors come out of the story about what made our code easy to modify, even after years of production:

⬩ A simple design, with no extra design elements—no ideas that weren't used yet but were expected to be used in the future.

✧ Automated tests, so we had confidence we would know if we accidentally changed the existing behavior of the system.

✧ Lots of practice in modifying the design, so when the time came to change the system, we weren't too afraid to try it.

With these elements in place—simple design, tests, and an attitude of constant refinement of the design—we experienced the flattened curve in Figure 3. A change that would have taken a few minutes before much coding had occurred took 30 minutes after we had been in production for two years. And I see projects spending days or weeks making the same sort of decision, rather than doing what they need to do today and trusting themselves to fix it tomorrow if they need to.

With this shift in assumption about the cost of change comes the opportunity to take an entirely different approach to software development. It is every bit as disciplined as other approaches, but it is disciplined along other dimensions. Instead of being careful to make big decisions early and little decisions later, we can create an approach to software development that makes each decision quickly, but backs each decision with automated tests, and that prepares you to improve the design of the software when you learn a better way to design it.

Creating such an approach won't be easy, though. We will have to reexamine our deepest assumptions about what makes for good software development. We can take the journey in stages. We'll start with a story, a story that will anchor everything else we do.

Chapter 6

Learning to Drive

We need to control the development of software by making many small adjustments, not by making a few large adjustments, kind of like driving a car. This means that we will need the feedback to know when we are a little off, we will need many opportunities to make corrections, and we will have to be able to make those corrections at a reasonable cost.

Now we have the general shape of the problem—the tremendous cost of risk, and the opportunity to manage that risk through options—and the resource needed to shape the solution: the freedom to make changes later in the cycle without significantly increased cost. Now we need to begin to bring the solution into focus. The first thing we need is a metaphor, a shared story that we can turn to in times of stress or decision to help keep us doing the right thing.

I can remember clearly the day I first began learning to drive. My mother and I were driving up Interstate 5 near Chico, California, a straight, flat stretch of road where the highway stretches right to the horizon. My mom had me reach over from the passenger seat and hold the steering wheel. She let me get the feel of how motion of the wheel affected the direction of the car. Then she told me, "Here's how you drive. Line the car up in the middle of the lane, straight toward the horizon."

I very carefully squinted straight down the road. I got the car smack dab in the middle of the lane, pointed right down the middle of the road. I was doing great. My mind wandered a little…

I jerked back to attention as the car hit the gravel. My mom (her courage now amazes me) gently got the car back straight on the road. Then she actually taught me about driving. "Driving is not about getting the car going in the right direction. Driving is about constantly paying attention, making a little correction this way, a little correction that way."

This is the paradigm for XP. There is no such thing as straight and level. Even if things seem to be going perfectly, you don't take your eyes off the road. Change is the only constant. Always be prepared to move a little this way, a little that way. Sometimes maybe you have to move in a completely different direction. That's life as a programmer.

Everything in software changes. The requirements change. The design changes. The business changes. The technology changes. The team changes. The team members change. The problem isn't change, per se, because change is going to happen; the problem, rather, is the inability to cope with change when it comes.

The driver of a software project is the customer. If the software doesn't do what they want it to do, you have failed. Of course, they don't know exactly what the software should do. That's why software development is like steering, not like getting the car pointed straight down the road. Our job as programmers is to give the customer a steering wheel and give them feedback about exactly where we are on the road.

The driving story also has a moral for the XP process itself. The four values—communication, simplicity, feedback, and courage—described in the next chapter tell us how software development should feel. However, the practices to achieve that feeling will be different from place to place and time to time and person to person. In steering your development process you adopt a simple set of practices that give you the feeling you want. As development continues, you are constantly aware of which practices enhance and which practices detract from your goal. Each practice is an experiment, to be followed until proven inadequate.

Chapter 7

Four Values

We will be successful when we have a style that celebrates a consistent set of values that serve both human and commercial needs: communication, simplicity, feedback, and courage.

Before we can reduce the story of learning to drive to a set of software development practices, we need some criteria for telling us if we're going in the right direction. It would be no good coming up with a style of development and then discovering that we didn't like it or it didn't work.

Short-term individual goals often conflict with long-term social goals. Societies have learned to deal with this problem by developing shared sets of values, backed up by myths, rituals, punishments, and rewards. Without these values, humans tend to revert to their own short-term best interest.

The four values of XP are:

✧ Communication
✧ Simplicity
✧ Feedback
✧ Courage

Communication

The first value of XP is communication. Problems with projects can invariably be traced back to somebody not talking to somebody else about something important. Sometimes a programmer doesn't tell someone else about a critical change in the design. Sometimes a programmer doesn't ask the customer the right question, so a critical domain decision is blown. Sometimes a manager doesn't ask a programmer the right question, and project progress is misreported.

Bad communication doesn't happen by chance. There are many circumstances that lead to a breakdown in communications. A programmer tells a manager bad news, and the manager punishes the programmer. A customer tells the programmer something important, and the programmer seems to ignore the information.

XP aims to keep the right communications flowing by employing many practices that can't be done without communicating. They are practices that make short-term sense, like unit testing, pair programming, and task estimation. The effect of testing, pairing, and estimating is that programmers and customers and managers have to communicate.

This doesn't mean that communications don't sometimes get clogged in an XP project. People get scared, make mistakes, get distracted. XP employs a coach whose job it is to notice when people aren't communicating and reintroduce them.

Simplicity

The second XP value is simplicity. The XP coach asks the team, "What is the simplest thing that could possibly work?"

Simplicity is not easy. It is the hardest thing in the world not to look toward the things you'll need to implement tomorrow and next week and next month. But compulsively thinking ahead is listening to the fear of the exponential cost of change curve. Sometimes the coach has to gently remind the team that they are listening to their fears, "Maybe you're so much smarter than I am that you can make all this complicated dynamically balancing tree stuff work. I would naively assume a linear search would work."

Greg Hutchinson writes:

> One person I was consulting to decided that we needed a general purpose dialog for displaying text. (OK, like we don't have enough already, but I digress.) We talked about the interface to

*this dialog and how it would work. The programmer decided
that this dialog should be fairly smart and modify its size and
the number of line breaks in the string based on the font size and
other variables. I asked this person how many programmers
needed this part currently. This programmer was the only one
that needed it. I suggested that we make the dialog not so smart
yet and make it work for their case (20 mins work), we could
make the Class and the interface known and always make it
smarter when a second case came along that needed those
requirements. I couldn't convince this programmer, and they
spent 2 days making this code. On the 3rd day even their
requirements had changed and they no longer needed this part.
2 man days gone on a project that was already tight. However,
please let me know if you could use this code.* (Source: e-mail.)

XP is making a bet. It is betting that it is better to do a simple thing today and pay a little more tomorrow to change it if it needs it, than to do a more complicated thing today that may never be used anyway.

Simplicity and communication have a wonderful mutually supporting relationship. The more you communicate, the clearer you can see exactly what needs to be done and the more confidence you have about what really doesn't need to be done. The simpler your system is, the less you have to communicate about, which leads to more complete communication, especially if you can simplify the system enough to require fewer programmers.

Feedback

The third value in XP is feedback. More coaching phrases are "Don't ask me, ask the system" and "Have you written a test case for that yet?" Concrete feedback about the current state of the system is absolutely priceless. Optimism is an occupational hazard of programming. Feedback is the treatment.

Feedback works at different time scales. First, feedback works at the scale of minutes and days. The programmers write unit tests for all the logic in the system that could possibly break. The programmers have minute-by-minute concrete feedback about the state of their system. When customers write new "stories" (descriptions of features), the programmers immediately estimate them, so the customers have concrete feedback about the quality of their stories. The person who tracks progress watches the completion of the tasks to give the whole team feedback about whether they are likely to finish everything they set out to do in a span of time.

Feedback also works at the scale of weeks and months. The customers and testers write functional tests for all the stories (think "simplified use cases") implemented by the system. They have concrete feedback about the current state of their system. The customers review the schedule every two or three weeks to see if the team's overall velocity matches the plan, and to adjust the plan. The system is put into production as soon as it makes sense, so the business can begin to "feel" what the system is like in action and discover how it can best be exploited.

Early production needs a little explanation. One of the strategies in the planning process is that the team puts the most valuable stories into production as soon as possible. This gives the programmers concrete feedback about the quality of their decisions and development process that never comes until the rubber meets the road. Some programmers have never lived with a system in production. How can they possibly learn to do a better job?

Most projects seem to have exactly the opposite strategy. The thinking seems to go, "As soon as the system is in production, you can no longer make 'interesting' changes, so keep the system in development as long as possible."

This is exactly backwards. "In development" is a temporary state, one that the system will only be in for a small percentage of its life. Far better to give the system independent life, to make it stand and breathe on its own. You are going to have to live with supporting production and developing new functionality simultaneously. Better to get used to juggling production and development sooner rather than later.

Concrete feedback works together with communication and simplicity. The more feedback you have, the easier it is to communicate. If someone has an objection to some code you have written and they hand you a test case that breaks it, that is worth a thousand hours of discussion about design aesthetics. If you are communicating clearly, you will know what to test and measure to learn about the system. Simple systems are easier to test. Writing the test gives you a focus for just how simple the system can be—until the tests run, you're not done, and when the tests all run, you're done.

Courage

Within the context of the first three values—communication, simplicity, and feedback—it's time to go like hell. If you aren't going at absolutely your top speed, somebody else will be, and they will eat your lunch.

Here is a story of courage in action. In the middle of iteration 8 of a 10-iteration engineering schedule (25 weeks out of 30) of the first release of the first large XP project, the team discovered a fundamental flaw in the architecture. The functional test scores had been rising nicely, but then had flattened out far below where they needed to be. Fixing one defect caused another one. The problem was an architectural flaw.

(For the curious, the system computed payroll. Entitlements represented things the company owed employees. Deductions represented things the employees owed other people. Some people had been using negative Entitlements when they should have been using positive Deductions.)

The team did exactly the right thing. When they discovered that there was no way forward, they fixed the flaw. This immediately broke half of the tests that had been running. A few days of concentrated effort later, however, and the tests scores were again headed toward completion. That took courage.

Another courageous move is throwing code away. You know how sometimes you work all day on something, and it isn't going very well, and the machine crashes? And how the next morning you come in and in half an hour reconstruct all of the previous day's work but clean and simple this time?

Use this. If the end of the day is coming and the code is a little out of control, toss it. Maybe save the test cases, if you like the interface you've designed, but maybe not. Maybe just start over from scratch.

Or maybe you have three design alternatives. So, code a day's worth of each alternative, just to see how they feel. Toss the code and start over on the most promising design.

XP's design strategy resembles a hill-climbing algorithm. You get a simple design, then you make it a little more complex, then a little simpler, then a little more complex. The problem with hill-climbing algorithms is reaching local optima, where no small change can improve the situation, but a large change could.

What is to say that you won't ever develop yourself into a corner? Courage. Every once in a while someone on the team will have a crazy idea that just might slash the complexity of the whole system. If they have courage, they'll try it out. It will work (sometimes). If they have courage, they'll put it into production. Now you're climbing a whole new hill.

If you don't have the first three values in place, courage by itself is just plain hacking (in the pejorative sense of that word). However, when combined with communication, simplicity, and concrete feedback, courage becomes extremely valuable.

Communication supports courage because it opens the possibility for more high-risk, high-reward experiments. "You don't like that? I hate that code. Let's see how much of it we can replace in an afternoon." Simplicity supports courage because you can afford to be much more courageous with a simple system. You are much less likely to break it unknowingly. Courage supports simplicity because as soon as you see the possibility of simplifying the system you try it. Concrete feedback supports courage because you feel much safer trying radical surgery on the code if you can push a button and see the tests turn green at the end (or not, in which case you throw the code away).

The Values in Practice

I asked the C3 team (that first big XP project I mentioned earlier) to tell me stories about their proudest moment on the project. I was hoping to get stories about big refactorings, or being saved by tests, or a happy customer. Instead, I got this:

> *The moment I was proudest of was when Eddie moved to a job closer to home, avoiding a two-hour daily commute, so he could spend more time with his family. The team gave him total respect. Nobody said a word against him leaving. Everybody just asked what they could do to help.*

This points to a deeper value, one that lies below the surface of the other four—respect. If members of a team don't care about each other and what they are doing, XP is doomed. So probably are most other approaches to writing software (or getting anything done), but XP is extremely sensitive to this. Given some basic compassion and interest, XP might provide some ongoing lubrication for all those pieces moving against each other. If members of a team don't care about the project, nothing can save it. Given some minimal passion, XP provides some positive feedback. This is not manipulative; it's just enjoying being part of something that works, instead of part of something that doesn't work.

All of this high-minded talk is well and good, but if there isn't some way to reduce it to practice, to reinforce it, to make the values a natural habit, then all we will have is yet another brave leap into the swamp of methodological good intentions. Next we have to have a more concrete guide leading us to practices that satisfy and embody the four values of communication, simplicity, feedback, and courage.

Chapter 8

Basic Principles

From the four values we derive a dozen or so basic principles to guide our new style. We will check proposed development practices to see how they measure up to these principles.

"Learning to Drive" reminds us to make lots of small changes and never take our eyes off the road. The four values—communication, simplicity, feedback, and courage—give us our criteria for a successful solution. However, the values are too vague to give us much help in deciding which practices to use. We need to distill the values into concrete principles we can use.

These principles will help us as we choose between alternatives. We will prefer an alternative that meets the principles more fully to one that doesn't. Each principle embodies the values. A value may be vague. One person's simple is another person's complex. A principle is more concrete. Either you have rapid feedback or you don't. Here are the fundamental principles:

- ✧ Rapid feedback
- ✧ Assume simplicity
- ✧ Incremental change
- ✧ Embracing change
- ✧ Quality work

Rapid feedback—Learning psychology teaches that the time between an action and its feedback is critical to learning. Animal experiments show that even small differences in the timing of feedback result in large differences in learning. A few seconds delay between stimulus and response and the mouse doesn't learn that the red button means food. So, one of the principles is to get feedback, interpret it, and put what is learned back into the system as quickly as possible. The business learns how the system can best contribute, and feeds back that learning in days or weeks instead of months or years. The programmers learn how best to design, implement and test the system, and feed back that learning in seconds or minutes instead of days, weeks, or months.

Assume simplicity—Treat every problem as if it can be solved with ridiculous simplicity. The time you save on the 98% of problems for which this is true will give you ridiculous resources to apply to the other 2%. In many ways, this is the hardest principle for programmers to swallow. We are traditionally told to plan for the future, to design for reuse. Instead, XP says to do a good job (tests, refactoring, communication) of solving today's job today and trust your ability to add complexity in the future where you need it. The economics of software as options favor this approach.

Incremental change—Big changes made all at once just don't work. Even in Switzerland, center of meticulous planning, where I live now, they don't try to make big changes. Any problem is solved with a series of the smallest changes that make a difference.

You'll find incremental change applied many ways in XP. The design changes a little at a time. The plan changes a little at a time. The team changes a little at a time. Even the adoption of XP must be taken in little steps.

Embracing change—The best strategy is the one that preserves the most options while actually solving your most pressing problem.

Quality work—Nobody likes working sloppy. Everybody likes doing a good job. Of the four project development variables—scope, cost, time, and quality—quality isn't really a free variable. The only possible values are "excellent" and "insanely excellent," depending on whether lives are at stake or not. Otherwise you don't enjoy your work, you don't work well, and the project goes down the drain.

Here are some less central principles. They still will help us decide what to do in specific situations.

- ⟡ Teach learning
- ⟡ Small initial investment
- ⟡ Play to win
- ⟡ Concrete experiments
- ⟡ Open, honest communication
- ⟡ Work with people's instincts, not against them
- ⟡ Accepted responsibility
- ⟡ Local adaptation
- ⟡ Travel light
- ⟡ Honest measurement

Teach learning—Rather than make a bunch of doctrinaire statements like "Thou must do testing like XYZ," we will focus on teaching strategies for learning how much testing you should do. Also how much design, and refactoring, and everything else you should do. Some ideas that we will state with certainty. There will be others that we don't have quite so much confidence in, and those we will state as strategies with which the reader can learn their own answers.

Small initial investment—Too many resources too early in a project is a recipe for disaster. Tight budgets force programmers and customers to pare requirements and approaches. The focus a tight budget generates encourages you to do a good job of everything you do. However, resources can be too tight. If you don't have the resources to solve even one interesting problem, then the system you create is guaranteed not to be interesting. If you have someone dictating scope, dates, quality, and cost, then you are unlikely to be able to navigate to a successful conclusion. Mostly, though, everyone can get by with fewer resources than they are comfortable with.

Play to win—It was always wonderful to watch John Wooden's UCLA basketball teams. They were usually crushing the opposition. However, even if the game was close going into the final minutes, UCLA was absolutely certain that they were going to win. After all, they had won so many, many times before. So, they were relaxed. They did what they needed to do. And they won again.

I remember an Oregon basketball game that provides a stark contrast. Oregon was playing a nationally ranked Arizona team that was destined to send four players to the NBA. At halftime, amazingly, Oregon was up by 12 points. Arizona couldn't do anything right, and Oregon's offense had them baffled. After the half, however, Oregon came out and tried to play as slowly as possible to reduce the number of points scored and preserve the victory. The strategy didn't work, of course. Arizona found ways to use their huge advantage in talent to win the game.

The difference is between playing to win and playing not to lose. Most software development I see is played not to lose. Lots of paper gets written. Lots of meetings are held. Everyone is trying to develop "by the book," not because it makes any particular sense, but because they want to be able to say at the end that it wasn't their fault, they were following the process. CYA.

Software development played to win does everything that helps the team to win and doesn't do anything that doesn't help to win.

Concrete experiments—Every time you make a decision and you don't test it, there is some probability that the decision is wrong. The more decisions you make, the more these risks compound. Therefore, the result of a design session should be a series of experiments addressing the questions raised during the session, not a finished design. The result of a discussion of requirements should also be a series of experiments. Every abstract decision should be tested.

Open, honest communication—This is such a motherhood statement that I almost left it out. Who wouldn't want to communicate openly and honestly? Everybody I visit, it seems. Programmers have to be able to explain the consequences of other people's decisions, "You violated encapsulation here and it really messed me up." They have to be able to tell each other where there are problems in the code. They have to be free to express their fears, and get support. They have to be free to deliver bad news to customers and management, to deliver it early, and not be punished.

If I see someone looking around to see who is listening before answering a question, I take it as a sign of deep trouble on the project. If there are personal matters to be discussed, I can understand the need for privacy. But which of two object models to use is not a matter that is helped by a "top secret" stamp.

Work with people's instincts, not against them—People like winning. People like learning. People like interacting with other people. People like being part of a team. People like being in control. People like being trusted. People like doing a good job. People like having their software work.

Paul Chisolm writes:

> *I was in a meeting, and the quality assurance wannabe manager suggested adding about half a dozen fields (to an online form already full of data no one ever used), not because the information would be useful downstream, but allegedly because filling out these additional fields would SAVE TIME. My reaction: I banged my head against the conference room table, like a Warner Brothers cartoon character who's just heard something unbelievable, and told him to stop lying to me. (To this day, I don't know if that was one of the least professional things I ever did, or one of the most professional. I have been told by an eye doctor to stop banging my head against things; it can cause retinas to detach.)* (Source: e-mail.)

It's been tricky, designing a process where following short-term self-interest also serves long-term team interest. You can expound all you want on how some practice or other is in everybody's best interest long-term, but when the pressure mounts, if the practice doesn't solve an immediate problem it will be discarded. If XP can't work with people's short-term interest, it is doomed to the outer methodological darkness.

Some folks really like this about XP, that it celebrates what programmers seem to do when left to their own devices, with just enough control to keep the whole process on track. One quote I remember was, "XP matches observations of programmers in the wild."

Accepted responsibility—No single action takes the life out of a team or a person more than being told what to do, especially if the job is clearly impossible. Primate dominance displays work only so long in getting people to act like they are going along. Along the way, a person told what to do will find a thousand ways of expressing their frustration, most of them to the detriment of the team and many of them to the detriment of the person.

The alternative is that responsibility be accepted, not given. This does not mean that you always do exactly what you feel like doing. You are part of a team, and if the team comes to the conclusion that a certain task needs doing, someone will choose to do it, no matter how odious.

Local adaptation—You have to adapt whatever you read in this book to your local conditions. This is an application of accepted responsibility to your development process. Adopting XP does not mean that I get to decide how you are going to develop. It means that you get to decide how to develop. I can tell you what I have found to work well. I can point out the consequences that I see from deviating. At the end of the day, however, this is your process. You have to decide on something today. You have to be aware of whether it still works tomorrow. You have to change and adapt. Don't read this thinking, "Finally, now I know how to develop." You should end up saying, "I have to decide all of this *and* program?" Yes, you do. But it's worth it.

Travel light—You can't expect to carry a lot of baggage and move fast. The artifacts we maintain should be:

- ✧ Few
- ✧ Simple
- ✧ Valuable

The XP team becomes intellectual nomads, always prepared to quickly pack up the tents and follow the herd. The herd in this case might be a design that wants to go a different direction than anticipated, or a customer that wants to go a different direction than anticipated, or a team member who leaves, or a technology that suddenly gets hot, or a business climate that shifts.

Like the nomads, the XP team gets used to traveling light. They don't carry much in the way of baggage except what they must have to keep producing value for the customer—tests and code.

Honest measurement—Our quest for control over software development has led us to measure, which is fine, but it has led us to measure at a level of detail that is not supported by our instruments. Better to say "This will take two weeks, more or less" than say, "14.176 hours," if you have no real way of estimating to this level of detail. We will also strive to choose metrics that have correlation to the way we want to work. For example, lines of code is a useless measurement in the face of code that shrinks when we learn better ways of programming.

Chapter 9

Back to Basics

We want to do everything we must do to have stable, predictable software development. But we don't have time for anything extra. The four basic activities of development are coding, testing, listening, and designing.

"Learning to Drive." Four values—communication, simplicity, feedback, and courage. A double handful of principles. Now we are ready to start building a discipline of software development. The first step is to decide on the scope. What is it that we will try to prescribe? What sorts of problems will we address and what sorts of problems will we ignore?

I remember when I first learned to program in BASIC. I had a couple of workbooks covering the fundamentals of programming. I went through them pretty quickly. When I had done that, I wanted to tackle a more challenging problem than the little exercises in the books. I decided I would write a Star Trek game, kind of like one I had played at the Lawrence Hall of Science in Berkeley, but cooler.

My process for writing the programs to solve the workbook exercises had been to stare at the problem for a few minutes, type in the code to solve it, then deal with whatever problems arose. So I sat confidently down to write my game. Nothing came. I had no idea how to write an application bigger than 20 lines. So I stepped away and I tried to write down the whole program on paper before typing it in. I got three lines written before I got stuck again.

I needed to do something beyond programming. But I didn't know what else to do.

So, what if we went back to that state, but in the light of experience? What would we do? We know we can't just "code till we're done." What activities would we add? What would we try to get out of each activity as we experienced it afresh?

Coding

At the end of the day, there has to be a program. So, I nominate coding as the one activity we know we can't do without. Whether you draw diagrams that generate code or you type at a browser, you are coding.

What is it that we want to get out of code? The most important thing is learning. The way I learn is to have a thought, then test it out to see if it is a good thought. Code is the best way I know of to do this. Code isn't swayed by the power and logic of rhetoric. Code isn't impressed by college degrees or large salaries. Code just sits there, happily doing exactly what you told it to do. If that isn't what you thought you told it to do, that's your problem.

When you code something up, you also have an opportunity to understand the best structure for the code. There are certain signs in the code that tell you that you don't yet understand the necessary structure.

Code also gives you a chance to communicate clearly and concisely. If you have an idea and explain it to me, I can easily misunderstand. If we code it together, though, I can see in the logic you write the precise shape of your ideas. Again, I see the shape of your ideas not as you see them in your head, but as they find expression to the outside world.

This communication easily turns into learning. I see your idea and I get one of my own. I have trouble expressing it to you, so I turn to code, also. Since it is a related idea, we use related code. You see that idea and have another.

Finally, code is the one artifact that development absolutely cannot live without. I've heard stories of systems where the source code was lost but they stayed in production. Sightings of such beasts has become increasingly rare, however. For a system to live, it must retain its source code.

Since we must have the source code, we should use it for as many of the purposes of software engineering as possible. It turns out that code can be used to communicate—expressing tactical intent, describing algorithms, pointing to spots for possible future expansion and contraction. Code can also be used to express tests, tests that both objectively test the operation of the system and provide a valuable operational specification of the system at all levels.

Testing

The English Positivist philosophers Locke, Berkeley, and Hume said that anything that can't be measured doesn't exist. When it comes to code, I agree with them completely. Software features that can't be demonstrated by automated tests simply don't exist. I am good at fooling myself into believing that what I wrote is what I meant. I am also good at fooling myself into believing that what I meant is what I should have meant. So I don't trust anything I write until I have tests for it. The tests give me a chance to think about what I want independent of how it will be implemented. Then the tests tell me if I implemented what I thought I implemented.

When most people think of automated tests, they think of testing functionality—that is, what numbers are computed. The more experience I get writing tests, the more I discover I can write tests for nonfunctional requirements—like performance or adherence of code to standards.

Erich Gamma coined the phrase "Test Infected" to describe people who won't code if they don't already have a test. The tests tell you when you are done—when the tests run, you are done coding for the moment. When you can't think of any tests to write that might break, you are completely done.

Tests are both a resource and a responsibility. You don't get to write just one test, make it run, and declare yourself finished. You are responsible for writing every test that you can imagine won't run immediately. After a while you will get good at reasoning about tests—if these two tests work, then you can safely conclude that this third test will work without having to write it. Of course, this is exactly the same kind of reasoning that leads to bugs in programs, so you have to be careful about it. If problems show up later and they would have been uncovered had you written that third test, you have to be prepared to learn the lesson and write that third test next time.

Most software ships without being developed with comprehensive automated tests. Automated tests clearly aren't essential. So why don't I leave testing out of my list of essential activities? I have two answers: one short-term and one long-term.

The long-term answer is that tests keep the program alive longer (if the tests are run and maintained). When you have the tests, you can make more changes longer than you can without the tests. If you keep writing the tests, your confidence in the system increases over time.

One of our principles is to work with human nature and not against it. If all you could make was a long-term argument for testing, you could forget about it. Some people would do it out of a sense of duty or because someone was watching over their shoulder. As soon as the attention wavered or the pressure increased, no new tests would get written, the tests that were written wouldn't be run, and the whole thing would fall apart. So, if we want to go with human nature and we want the tests, we have to find a short-term selfish reason for testing.

Fortunately, there is a short-term reason to write tests. Programming when you have the tests is more fun than programming when you don't. You code with so much more confidence. You never have to entertain those nagging thoughts of "Well, this is the right thing to do right now, but I wonder what I broke." Push the button. Run all the tests. If the light turns green, you are ready to go to the next thing with renewed confidence.

I caught myself doing this in a public programming demonstration. Every time I would turn from the audience to begin programming again, I would push my testing button. I hadn't changed any code. Nothing in the environment had changed. I just wanted a little jolt of confidence. Seeing that the tests still ran gave me that.

Programming and testing together is also faster than just programming. I didn't expect this effect when I started, but I certainly noticed it and have heard it reported by lots of other people. You might gain productivity for half an hour by not testing. Once you have gotten used to testing, though, you will quickly notice the difference in productivity. The gain in productivity comes from a reduction in the time spent debugging—you no longer spend an hour looking for a bug, you find it in minutes. Sometimes you just can't get a test to work. Then you likely have a much bigger problem, and you need to step back and make sure your tests are right, or whether the design needs refinement.

However, there is a danger. Testing done badly becomes a set of rose-colored glasses. You gain false confidence that your system is okay because the tests all run. You move on, little realizing that you have left a trap behind you, armed and ready to spring the next time you come that way.

The trick with testing is finding the level of defects you are willing to tolerate. If you can stand one customer complaint per month, then invest in testing and improve your testing process until you get to that level. Then, using that standard of testing, move forward as if the system is fine if the tests all run.

Looking ahead just a little, we will have two sets of tests. We will have unit tests written by the programmers to convince themselves that their programs work the way they think the programs work. We will also have functional tests written by (or at least specified by) the customers to convince themselves that the system as a whole works the way they think the system as a whole should work.

There are two audiences for the tests. The programmers need to make their confidence concrete in the form of tests so everyone else can share in their confidence. The customers need to prepare a set of tests that represent their confidence, "Well, I guess if you can compute all of these cases, the system must work."

Listening

Programmers don't know anything. Rather, programmers don't know anything that business people think is interesting. Hey, if those business people could do without programmers, they would throw us out in a second.

Where am I going with this? Well, if you resolve to test, you have to get the answers from somewhere. Since you (as a programmer) don't know anything, you have to ask someone else. They will tell you what the expected answers are, and what some of the unusual cases are from a business perspective.

If you are going to ask questions, then you'd better be prepared to listen to the answers. So listening is the third activity in software development.

Programmers must listen in the large, too. They listen to what the customer says the business problem is. They help the customer to understand what is hard and what is easy, so it is an active kind of listening. The feedback they provide helps the customer understand their business problems better.

Just saying, "You should listen to each other and to the customer," doesn't help much. People try that and it doesn't work. We have to find a way to structure the communication so that the things that have to be communicated get communicated when they need to be communicated and in the amount of detail they need to be communicated. Similarly, the rules we develop also have to discourage communication that doesn't help, that is done before what is to be communicated is really understood, or that is done in such great detail as to conceal the important part of the communication.

Designing

Why can't you just listen, write a test case, make it run, listen, write a test case, make it run indefinitely? Because we know it doesn't work that way. You can do that for a while. In a forgiving language you may even be able to do that for a long while. Eventually, though, you get stuck. The only way to make the next test case run is to break another. Or the only way to make the test case run is far more trouble than it is worth. Entropy claims another victim.

The only way to avoid this is to design. Designing is creating a structure that organizes the logic in the system. Good design organizes the logic so that a change in one part of the system doesn't always require a change in another part of the system. Good design ensures that every piece of logic in the system has one and only one home. Good design puts the logic near the data it operates on. Good design allows the extension of the system with changes in only one place.

Bad design is just the opposite. One conceptual change requires changes to many parts of the system. Logic has to be duplicated. Eventually, the cost of a bad design becomes overwhelming. You just can't remember any more where all the implicitly linked changes have to take place. You can't add new function without breaking existing function.

Complexity is another source of bad design. If a design requires four layers of indirection to find out what is really happening, and if those layers don't provide any particular functional or explanatory purpose, then the design is bad.

- -

So, the final activity we have to structure in our new discipline is designing. We have to provide a context in which good designs are created, bad designs are fixed, and the current design is learned by everyone who needs to learn it.

As you'll see in the following chapters, how XP achieves design is quite different from how many software processes achieve design. Design is part of the daily business of all programmers in XP in the midst of their coding. But regardless of the strategy used to achieve it, the activity of design is not an option. It must be given serious thought for software development to be effective.

Conclusion

So you code because if you don't code, you haven't done anything. You test because if you don't test, you don't know when you are done coding. You listen because if you don't listen you don't know what to code or what to test. And you design so you can keep coding and testing and listening indefinitely. That's it. Those are the activities we have to help structure:

- ✦ Coding
- ✦ Testing
- ✦ Listening
- ✦ Designing

Section 2

The Solution

Now we have set the stage. We know what problem we have to solve, namely deciding how the basic activities of software development should take place—coding, testing, listening, and designing. We have a set of guiding values and principles to guide us as we choose strategies for each of these activities. And we have the flattened cost curve as our ace in the hole to simplify the strategies we choose.

Chapter 10

A Quick Overview

We will rely on the synergies between simple practices, practices that often were abandoned decades ago as impractical or naïve.

The raw materials of our new software development discipline are

- ✧ The story about learning to drive
- ✧ The four values—communication, simplicity, feedback, and courage
- ✧ The principles
- ✧ The four basic activities—coding, testing, listening, and designing

Our job is to structure the four activities. Not only do we have to structure the activities, we have to do it in light of the long list of sometimes contradictory principles. And at the same time we have to try to improve the economic performance of software development enough so that someone will listen.

No problem.

Er …

As the purpose of this book is to explain how this could possibly work, I will quickly explain the major areas of practice in XP. In the next chapter, we will see how such ridiculously simple solutions could possibly work. Where a practice is weak, the strengths of other practices will cover for the weakness. Later chapters will cover some of the topics in more detail.

First, here are all the practices:

- *The Planning Game*—Quickly determine the scope of the next release by combining business priorities and technical estimates. As reality overtakes the plan, update the plan.
- *Small releases*—Put a simple system into production quickly, then release new versions on a very short cycle.
- *Metaphor*—Guide all development with a simple shared story of how the whole system works.
- *Simple design*—The system should be designed as simply as possible at any given moment. Extra complexity is removed as soon as it is discovered.
- *Testing*—Programmers continually write unit tests, which must run flawlessly for development to continue. Customers write tests demonstrating that features are finished.
- *Refactoring*—Programmers restructure the system without changing its behavior to remove duplication, improve communication, simplify, or add flexibility.
- *Pair programming*—All production code is written with two programmers at one machine.
- *Collective ownership*—Anyone can change any code anywhere in the system at any time.
- *Continuous integration*—Integrate and build the system many times a day, every time a task is completed.
- *40-hour week*—Work no more than 40 hours a week as a rule. Never work overtime a second week in a row.
- *On-site customer*—Include a real, live user on the team, available full-time to answer questions.
- *Coding standards*—Programmers write all code in accordance with rules emphasizing communication through the code.

In this chapter we will quickly summarize what is involved in executing each practice. In the next chapter (How Could This Work?) we will examine the connections between the practices that allow the weaknesses of one practice to be overcome by the strengths of other practices.

- -

The Planning Game

Neither business considerations nor technical considerations should be paramount. Software development is always an evolving dialog between the possible and the desirable. The nature of the dialog is that it changes both what is seen to be possible and what is seen to be desirable.

Business people need to decide about

- Scope—How much of a problem must be solved for the system to be valuable in production? The business person is in a position to understand how much is not enough and how much is too much.
- Priority—If you could only have A or B at first, which one do you want? The business person is in a position to determine this, much more so than a programmer.
- Composition of releases—How much or how little needs to be done before the business is better off with the software than without it? The programmer's intuition about this question can be wildly wrong.
- Dates of releases—What are important dates at which the presence of the software (or some of the software) would make a big difference?

Business can't make these decisions in a vacuum. Development needs to make the technical decisions that provide the raw material for the business decisions.

Technical people decide about

- Estimates—How long will a feature take to implement?
- Consequences—There are strategic business decisions that should be made only when informed about the technical consequences. Choice of a database is a good example. Business might rather work with a huge company than a startup, but a factor of 2 in productivity may make the extra risk or discomfort worth it. Or not. Development needs to explain the consequences.
- Process—How will the work and the team be organized? The team needs to fit the culture in which it will operate, but you

should write software well rather than preserve the irrationality of an enclosing culture.

✧ Detailed scheduling—Within a release, which stories will be done first? The programmers need the freedom to schedule the riskiest segments of development first, to reduce the overall risk of the project. Within that constraint, they still tend to move business priorities earlier in the process, reducing the chance that important stories will have to be dropped toward the end of the development of a release.

Small Releases

Every release should be as small as possible, containing the most valuable business requirements. The release has to make sense as a whole—that is, you can't implement half a feature and ship it, just to make the release cycle shorter.

It is far better to plan a month or two at a time than six months or a year at a time. A company shipping bulky software to customers might not be able to release this often. They should still reduce their cycle as much as possible.

Metaphor

Each XP software project is guided by a single overarching metaphor. Sometimes the metaphor is "naive," like a contract management system that is spoken of in terms of contracts and customers and endorsements. Sometimes the metaphor needs a little explanation, like saying the computer should appear as a desktop, or that pension calculation is like a spreadsheet. These are all metaphors, though, because we don't literally mean "the system is a spreadsheet." The metaphor just helps everyone on the project understand the basic elements and their relationships.

The words used to identify technical entities should be consistently taken from the chosen metaphor. As development proceeds and the metaphor matures, the whole team will find new inspiration from examining the metaphor.

The metaphor in XP replaces much of what other people call "architecture." The problem with calling the 10,000-meter view of the system an architecture is that architectures don't necessarily push the system into any sense of cohesion. An architecture is the big boxes and connections.

You could say, "Of course architecture badly done is bad." We need to emphasize the goal of architecture, which is to give everyone a coherent story within which to work, a story that can easily be shared by the business and technical folks. By asking for a metaphor we are likely to get an architecture that is easy to communicate and elaborate.

Simple Design

The right design for the software at any given time is the one that

1. Runs all the tests.
2. Has no duplicated logic. Be wary of hidden duplication like parallel class hierarchies.
3. States every intention important to the programmers.
4. Has the fewest possible classes and methods.

Every piece of design in the system must be able to justify its existence on these terms. Edward Tufte[1] has an exercise for graphic designers—design a graph however you want. Then, erase as long as you don't remove any information. Whatever is left when you can't erase any more is the right design for the graph. Simple design is like this—take out any design element that you can without violating rules 1, 2, and 3.

This is opposite advice from what you generally hear: "Implement for today, design for tomorrow." If you believe that the future is uncertain, and you believe that you can cheaply change your mind, then putting in functionality on speculation is crazy. Put in what you need when you need it.

Testing

Any program feature without an automated test simply doesn't exist. Programmers write unit tests so that their confidence in the operation of the program can become part of the program itself. Customers write functional tests so that their confidence in the operation of the program

---

1. Edward Tufte, *The Visual Display of Quantitative Information*, Graphics Press, 1992.

can become part of the program, too. The result is a program that becomes more and more confident over time—it becomes more capable of accepting change, not less.

You don't have to write a test for every single method you write, only production methods that could possibly break. Sometimes you just want to find out if something is possible. You go explore for half an hour. Yes, it is possible. Now you throw away your code and start over with tests.

Refactoring

When implementing a program feature, the programmers always ask if there is a way of changing the existing program to make adding the feature simple. After they have added a feature, the programmers ask if they now can see how to make the program simpler, while still running all of the tests. This is called refactoring.

Note that this means that sometimes you do more work than absolutely necessary to get a feature running. But in working this way, you ensure that you can add the next feature with a reasonable amount of effort, and the next, and the next. You don't refactor on speculation, though; you refactor when the system asks you to. When the system requires that you duplicate code, it is asking for refactoring.

If a programmer sees a one-minute ugly way to get a test working and a ten-minute way to get it working with a simpler design, the correct choice is to spend the ten minutes. Fortunately, you can make even radical changes to the design of a system in small, low-risk steps:

Pair Programming

All production code is written with two people looking at one machine, with one keyboard and one mouse.

There are two roles in each pair. One partner, the one with the keyboard and the mouse, is thinking about the best way to implement this method right here. The other partner is thinking more strategically:

◇ Is this whole approach going to work?
◇ What are some other test cases that might not work yet?
◇ Is there some way to simplify the whole system so the current problem just disappears?

Pairing is dynamic. If two people pair in the morning, in the afternoon they might easily be paired with other folks. If you have responsibility for a task in an area that is unfamiliar to you, you might ask someone with recent experience to pair with you. More often, anyone on the team will do as a partner.

Collective Ownership

Anybody who sees an opportunity to add value to any portion of the code is required to do so at any time.

Contrast this to two other models of code ownership—no ownership and individual ownership. In the olden days, nobody owned any particular piece of code. If someone wanted to change some code, they did it to suit their own purpose, whether it fit well with what was already there or not. The result was chaos, especially with objects where the relationship between a line of code over here and a line of code over there was not easy to determine statically. The code grew quickly, but it also quickly grew unstable.

To get control of this situation, individual code ownership arose. The only person who could change a piece of code was its official owner. Anyone else who saw that the code needed changing had to submit their request to the owner. The result of strict ownership is that the code diverges from the team's understanding, as people are reluctant to interrupt the code owner. After all, they need the change now, not later. So the code remains stable, but it doesn't evolve as quickly as it should. Then the owner leaves ....

In XP, everybody takes responsibility for the whole of the system. Not everyone knows every part equally well, although everyone knows something about every part. If a pair is working and they see an opportunity to improve the code, they go ahead and improve it if it makes their life easier.

Continuous Integration

Code is integrated and tested after a few hours—a day of development at most. One simple way to do this is to have a machine dedicated to integration. When the machine is free, a pair with code to integrate sits down, loads the current release, loads their changes (checking for and resolving any collisions), and runs the tests until they pass (100% correct).

Integrating one set of changes at a time works well because it is obvious who should fix a test that fails—we should, since we must have broken it, since the last pair left the tests at 100%. And if we can't get the tests to run at 100%, we should throw away what we did and start over, since we obviously didn't know enough to be programming that feature (although we likely do know enough now).

40-Hour Week

I want to be fresh and eager every morning, and tired and satisfied every night. On Friday, I want to be tired and satisfied enough that I feel good about two days to think about something other than work. Then on Monday I want to come in full of fire and ideas.

Whether this translates into precisely 40 hours per week at the work site is not terribly important. Different people have different tolerances for work. One person might be able to put in 35 concentrated hours, another 45. But no one can put in 60 hours a week for many weeks and still be fresh and creative and careful and confident. Don't do that.

Overtime is a symptom of a serious problem on the project. The XP rule is simple—you can't work a second week of overtime. For one week, fine, crank and put in some extra hours. If you come in Monday and say, "To meet our goals, we'll have to work late again," then you already have a problem that can't be solved by working more hours.

A related issue is vacation. Europeans often take vacations of two, three, or four straight weeks. Americans seldom take more than a few days at a time. If it were my company, I would insist that people take a two-week vacation every year, with at least another week or two available for shorter breaks.

On-Site Customer

A real customer must sit with the team, available to answer questions, resolve disputes, and set small-scale priorities. By "real customer" I mean someone who will really use the system when it is in production. If you are building a customer service system, the customer will be a customer service representative. If you are building a bond trading system, the customer will be a bond trader.

The big objection to this rule is that real users of the system under development are too valuable to give to the team. Managers will have to decide which is more valuable—having the software working sooner and better or having the output of one or two people. If having the system doesn't bring more value to the business than having one more person working, perhaps the system shouldn't be built.

And it's not as if the customer on the team can't get any work done. Even programmers can't generate 40 hours of questions each and every week. The on-site customer will have the disadvantage of being physically separated from other customers, but they will likely have time to do their normal work.

The downside of an on-site customer is if they spend hundreds of hours helping the programmers and then the project is canceled. Then you have lost the work they did, and you have also lost the work they could have done if they hadn't been contributing to a failing project. XP does everything possible to make sure that the project doesn't fail.

I worked on one project where we were grudgingly given a real customer, but "only for a little while." After the system shipped successfully and was obviously able to continue evolving, the managers on the customer side gave us three real customers. The company could have gotten more value out of the system with more business contribution.

Coding Standards

If you are going to have all these programmers changing from this part of the system to that part of the system, swapping partners a couple of times a day, and refactoring each other's code constantly, you simply cannot afford to have different sets of coding practices. With a little practice, it should become impossible to say who on the team wrote what code.

The standard should call for the least amount of work possible, consistent with the Once and Only Once rule (no duplicate code). The standard should emphasize communication. Finally, the standard must be adopted voluntarily by the whole team.

Chapter 11

How Could This Work?

The practices support each other. The weakness of one is covered by the strengths of others.

Wait just a doggone minute. None of the practices described above is unique or original. They have all been used for as long as there have been programs to write. Most of these practices have been abandoned for more complicated, higher overhead practices, as their weaknesses have become apparent. Why isn't XP a simplistic approach to software? Before we go on, we had better convince ourselves that these simple practices won't kill us, just as they killed software projects decades ago.

The collapse of the exponential change cost curve brings all these practices back into play again. Each of the practices still has the same weaknesses as before, but what if those weaknesses were now made up for by the strengths of other practices? We might be able to get away with doing things simply.

This chapter presents another look at the practices, but this time focused on what usually makes the practice untenable, and showing how the other practices keep the bad effects of each from overwhelming the project. This chapter also shows how the whole XP story could possibly work.

The Planning Game

You couldn't possibly start development with only a rough plan. You couldn't constantly update the plan—that would take too long and upset the customers. Unless:

- ✧ The customers did the updating of the plan themselves, based on estimates provided by the programmers.
- ✧ You had enough of a plan at the beginning to give the customers a rough idea of what was possible over the next couple of years.
- ✧ You made short releases so any mistake in the plan would have a few weeks or months of impact at most.
- ✧ Your customer was sitting with the team, so they could spot potential changes and opportunities for improvement quickly.

Then perhaps you could start development with a simple plan, and continually refine it as you went along.

Short Releases

You couldn't possibly go into production after a few months. You certainly couldn't make new releases of the system on cycles ranging from daily to every couple of months. Unless:

- ✧ The Planning Game helped you work on the most valuable stories, so even a small system had business value.
- ✧ You were integrating continuously, so the cost of packaging a release was minimal.
- ✧ Your testing reduced the defect rate enough so you didn't have to go through a lengthy test cycle before allowing software to escape.
- ✧ You could make a simple design, sufficient for this release, not for all time.

Then perhaps you could make small releases, starting soon after development begins.

Metaphor

You couldn't possibly start development with just a metaphor. There isn't enough detail there, and besides, what if you're wrong? Unless:

- ✧ You quickly have concrete feedback from real code and tests about whether the metaphor is working in practice.
- ✧ Your customer is comfortable talking about the system in terms of the metaphor.
- ✧ You refactor to continually refine your understanding of what the metaphor means in practice.

Then perhaps you could start development with just a metaphor.

Simple Design

You couldn't possibly have just enough design for today's code. You would design yourself into a corner and then you'd be stuck, unable to continue evolving the system. Unless:

- ✧ You were used to refactoring, so making changes was not a worry.
- ✧ You had a clear overall metaphor so you were sure future design changes would tend to follow a convergent path.
- ✧ You were programming with a partner, so you were confident you were making a simple design, not a stupid design.

Then perhaps you could get away with doing the best possible job of making a design for today.

Testing

You couldn't possibly write all those tests. It would take too much time. Programmers won't write tests. Unless:

- ✧ The design is as simple as it can be, so writing tests isn't all that difficult.
- ✧ You are programming with a partner, so if you can't think of another test your partner can, and if your partner feels like blowing off the tests, you can gently rip the keyboard away.

- ⬥ You feel good when you see the tests all running.
- ⬥ Your customer feels good about the system when they see all of their tests running.

Then perhaps programmers and customers will write tests. Besides, if you don't write automated tests, the rest of XP doesn't work nearly as well.

Refactoring

You couldn't possibly refactor the design of the system all the time. It would take too long, it would be too hard to control, and it would most likely break the system. Unless:

- ⬥ You are used to collective ownership, so you don't mind making changes wherever they are needed.
- ⬥ You have coding standards, so you don't have to reformat before refactoring.
- ⬥ You program in pairs, so you are more likely to have the courage to tackle a tough refactoring, and you are less likely to break something.
- ⬥ You have a simple design, so the refactorings are easier.
- ⬥ You have the tests, so you are less likely to break something without knowing it.
- ⬥ You have continuous integration, so if you accidentally break something at a distance, or one of your refactorings conflicts with someone else's work, you know in a matter of hours.
- ⬥ You are rested, so you have more courage and are less likely to make mistakes.

Then perhaps you could refactor whenever you saw the chance to make the system simpler, or reduce duplication, or communicate more clearly.

Pair Programming

You can't possibly write all the production code in pairs. It will be too slow. What if two people don't get along? Unless:

- The coding standards reduce the picayune squabbles.
- Everyone is fresh and rested, reducing further the chance of unprofitable … uh … discussions.
- The pairs write tests together, giving them a chance to align their understanding before tackling the meat of the implementation.
- The pairs have the metaphor to ground their decisions about naming and basic design.
- The pairs are working within a simple design, so they can both understand what is going on.

Then perhaps you could write all production code in pairs. Besides, if people program solo they are more likely to make mistakes, more likely to overdesign, and more likely to blow off the other practices, particularly under pressure.

Collective Ownership

You couldn't possibly have everybody potentially changing anything anywhere. Folks would be breaking stuff left and right, and the cost of integration would go up dramatically. Unless:

- You integrate after a short enough time, so the chances of conflicts go down.
- You write and run the tests, so the chance of breaking things accidentally goes down.
- You pair program, so you are less likely to break code, and programmers learn faster what they can profitably change.
- You adhere to coding standards, so you don't get into the dreaded Curly Brace Wars.

Then perhaps you could have anyone change code anywhere in the system when they see the chance to improve it. Besides, without collective ownership the rate of evolution of the design slows dramatically.

Continuous Integration

You couldn't possibly integrate after only a few hours of work. Integration takes far too long and there are too many conflicts and chances to accidentally break something. Unless:

⬥ You can run the tests quickly so you know you haven't broken anything.

⬥ You program in pairs, so there are half as many streams of changes to integrate.

⬥ You refactor, so there are more smaller pieces, reducing the chance of conflicts.

Then perhaps you could integrate after a few hours. Besides, if you don't integrate quickly then the chance of conflicts rises and the cost of integration goes up steeply.

40-Hour Week

You couldn't possibly work 40-hour weeks. You can't create enough business value in 40 hours. Unless:

⬥ The Planning Game is feeding you more valuable work to do.

⬥ The combination of the Planning Game and testing reduces the frequency of nasty surprises, where you have more to do than you thought.

⬥ The practices as a whole help you program at top speed, so there isn't any faster you can go.

Then perhaps you could produce enough business value in 40-hour weeks. Besides, if the team doesn't stay fresh and energetic, then they won't be able to execute the rest of the practices.

On-Site Customer

You couldn't possibly have a real customer on the team, sitting there full-time. They can produce far more value for the business elsewhere. Unless:

⋄ They can produce value for the project by writing functional tests.

⋄ They can produce value for the project by making small-scale priority and scope decisions for the programmers.

Then perhaps they can produce more value for the company by contributing to the project. Besides, if the team doesn't include a customer, they will have to add risk to the project by planning further in advance and coding without knowing exactly what tests they have to satisfy and what tests they can ignore.

Coding Standards

You couldn't possibly ask the team to code to a common standard. Programmers are deeply individualistic, and would quit rather than put their curly braces somewhere else. Unless:

⋄ The whole of XP makes them more likely to be members of a winning team.

Then perhaps they would be willing to bend their style a little. Besides, without coding standards the additional friction slows pair programming and refactoring significantly.

Conclusion

Any one practice doesn't stand well on its own (with the possible exception of testing). They require the other practices to keep them in balance. Figure 4 is a diagram that summarizes the practices. A line

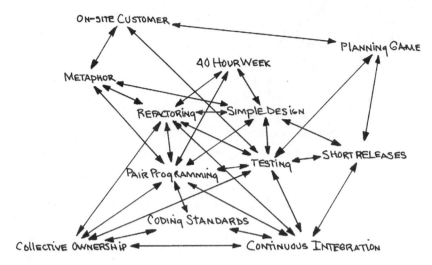

FIGURE 4. The practices support each other

between two practices means that the two practices reinforce each other. I didn't want to present this picture first, because it makes XP look complicated. The individual pieces are simple. The richness comes from the interactions of the parts.

Chapter 12

Management Strategy

We will manage the overall project using business basics—phased delivery, quick and concrete feedback, clear articulation of the business needs of the system, and specialists for special tasks.

The management dilemma: On the one hand, you would like the manager to make all the decisions. There is no communication overhead, because there is only one person. There is one person to be responsible to upper management. There is one person to have the vision. No one else needs to know about it, because all the decisions come from one person.

We know this strategy doesn't work, because no one person knows enough to do a good job of making all the decisions. Management strategies that are balanced toward centralized control are also difficult to execute, because they require lots of overhead on the part of those being managed.

On the other hand, the opposite strategy doesn't work. You can't just let everyone go off and do what they want without any oversight. People inevitably get off on tangents. Someone needs to have a bigger view of the project, and to be able to influence the project when it gets off course.

Once again, we can fall back on the principles to help us navigate between these two extremes:

✧ Accepted responsibility—suggests that it is the manager's job to highlight what needs to be done, not to assign work.

◇ Quality work—suggests that the relationship between managers and programmers needs to be based on trust, because the programmers want to do a good job. On the other hand, this doesn't mean the manager does nothing. However, there is a big difference between "I am trying to get these guys to do a decent job" and "I get to help these guys do an even better job."

◇ Incremental change—suggests that the manager provides guidance all along, not a big policy manual at the beginning.

◇ Local adaptation—suggests that the manager needs to take the lead in adapting XP to local conditions, to be aware of how the XP culture clashes with the company culture and to find a way to resolve the misfit.

◇ Travel light—suggests that the manager doesn't impose a lot of overhead—long all-hands meetings, lengthy status reports. Whatever the manager requires of the programmers shouldn't take much time to fulfill.

◇ Honest measurement—suggests that whatever metrics the manager gathers should be at realistic levels of accuracy. Don't try to account for every second if your watch only has a minute hand.

The strategy that emerges from this evaluation is more like decentralized decision making than centralized control. The manager's job is to run the Planning Game, to collect metrics, to make sure the metrics are seen by those whose work is being measured, and occasionally to intervene in situations that can't be resolved in a distributed way.

Metrics

The basic XP management tool is the metric. For example, the ratio between estimated development time and calendar time is the basic measure for running the Planning Game. It lets the team set the Project Velocity. If the ratio rises (less calendar time for a given estimated amount of development), it can mean that the team process is working well. Or, it can mean that the team isn't doing enough besides fulfilling requirements (like refactoring and pairing), and that a price will be paid long-term.

The medium of the metric is the Big Visible Chart. Rather than send e-mail to everyone, which they learn to ignore, the manager periodically (no less than weekly) updates a prominent chart. This is often all the intervention that is needed. You think there aren't enough tests being written? Put a chart of the number of tests up, and update it every day.

Don't have too many metrics, and be prepared to retire metrics that have served their purpose. Three or four measures are typically all a team can stand at one time.

Metrics tend to go stale over time. In particular, any metric that is approaching 100% is likely to be useless. For unit test scores, which must be 100%, this advice doesn't apply, but then the unit test score is more like an assumption than a metric. You can't count on 97% functional test scores to mean that you have 3% of the effort remaining, however. If a metric gets close to 100%, replace it with another that starts comfortably down in the single digits.

This is not to suggest that you can manage an XP project "by the numbers." Instead, the numbers are a way of gently and noncoercively communicating the need for change. The XP manager's most sensitive barometer of the need for change is awareness of his or her own feelings, physical and emotional. If your stomach knots when you get in the car in the morning, something is wrong with your project and it's your job to effect the change.

Coaching

What most folks think of as management is divided into two roles in XP: the coach and the tracker (these may or may not be filled by the same person). Coaching is primarily concerned with the technical execution (and evolution) of the process. The ideal coach is a good communicator, not easily panicked, technically skilled (although this is not an absolute requirement), and confident. Often, as coach you want to use the person who on other teams would have been the lead programmer or system architect. However, the coach role in XP is very different.

The phrases "lead programmer" and "system architect" conjure up visions of isolated geniuses making the important decisions on the project. The coach is just the opposite. The measure of a coach is how few technical decisions he or she makes: The job is to get everybody else making good decisions.

The coach doesn't take responsibility for many development tasks. Rather, the job duties are as follows:

◇ Be available as a development partner, particularly for new programmers beginning to take responsibility or for difficult technical tasks.

◇ See long-term refactoring goals, and encourage small-scale refactorings to address parts of these goals.

◇ Help programmers with individual technical skills, like testing, formatting, and refactoring.

◇ Explain the process to upper-level managers.

But perhaps the most important job for the coach is the acquisition of toys and food. XP projects seem to attract toys. Lots are of the ordinary brain-teaser type recommended by lateral thinking consultants everywhere. But every once in a while the coach will have the opportunity to profoundly influence development by buying just the right toy, and staying alive to this possibility is one of the coach's greatest responsibilities. For example, on the Chrysler C3 project, design meetings were going on for hours without resolution. So I bought an ordinary kitchen timer and decreed that no design meeting could be longer than 10 minutes. I don't believe the timer was ever used, but its visible presence reminded everyone to be aware of when a discussion had ceased being useful and had turned into a process for avoiding going and writing some code to get the answer for sure.

Food, also, is a hallmark of XP projects. There is something powerful about breaking bread with someone. You have an entirely different discussion with them if you are chewing at the same time. So XP projects always have food lying around. (I particularly recommend Frigor Noir chocolate bars if you can find them, but some projects seem to survive on Twizzler licorice sticks. You're welcome to develop your own local menu.)

Rob Mee writes:

> *You know, these test suites are quite insidious. On my team, we reward ourselves with food and beverage. At 2:45: "If we're back at 100% by 3:00 we can have tea and a snack." Of course, we have the snack anyway, even if it takes us until 3:15. However,*

we almost never get the snack until the tests do run—having the
accomplishment behind us makes the break a little party.
(Source: e-mail.)

Tracking

Tracking is the other major component of management in XP. You can make all the estimates you want, but if you don't measure what really happens against what you predicted would happen, you won't ever learn.

It is the job of the tracker to gather whatever metrics are being tracked at the moment and make sure the team is aware of what was actually measured (and reminded of what was predicted or desired).

Running the Planning Game is a part of tracking. The tracker needs to know the rules of the game cold and be prepared to enforce them even in emotional situations (planning is always emotional).

Tracking needs to happen without lots of overhead. If the person gathering actual development time is asking programmers for their status twice a day, the programmers will soon run away rather than face the interruption. Instead, the tracker should experiment with just how little measurement they can do and still be effective. Gathering real development data twice a week is plenty. More measurement probably won't give you better results.

Intervention

Managing an XP team isn't all fetching donuts and tossing Frisbees. There are times when problems simply can't be solved by the emergent brilliance of the team, encouraged by a loving and watchful manager. At times like this, the XP manager must be comfortable stepping in, making decisions—even unpopular ones—and seeing the consequences through to the end.

First, though, the manager must search carefully to discover if there was something they should have been aware of or done earlier to have avoided the problem entirely. The time for intervention is not the time for donning white armor and leaping on a charger. Rather, it is a time to come to the team and say, "I don't know how I let it get like this, but now I have to do XXX." Humility is the rule of the day for an intervention.

One of the matters serious enough for intervention is personnel changes. If a team member just isn't working out, the manager needs to ask them to leave. And decisions like this are better done sooner rather than later. As soon as you can't think of any scenario in which the offender would be a help rather than a hindrance, you should make the move. Waiting will only make the problem worse.

A slightly more pleasant duty is intervening when the team's process needs changing. It isn't the manager's job to dictate what is to change and how, generally, but to point out the need for change. The team should come up with one or more experiments to run. Then the manager reports back on the measured changes caused by the experiment.

The final interventionist duty of the manager is killing the project. The team would likely never quit on their own. But the day will come when further engineering investment in the current system is less attractive than some other alternative, like starting a replacement project. The manager is responsible for being aware of when this threshold has been crossed and for informing upper management of the need for the change.

Chapter 13

Facilities Strategy

We will create an open workspace for our team, with small private spaces around the periphery and a common programming area in the middle.

About Figure 5, Ron Jeffries writes:

This picture shows the DaimlerChrysler C3 Payroll team's work area. Two large tables each hold six development machines. Programmer pairs sit at any machine that's available to do their work. (This picture was not posed: they really do work together like this. The photographer was working with Chet, at the back table with his back to the camera.)

The two visible walls are paved with whiteboards, showing Functional Tests needing attention, planned CRC sessions, and the Iteration Plan on the back board. The sheets of paper at the top of the boards on the left are little signs containing the group's XP rules.

The walls to the right and below the camera are lined with little cubbies, just large enough for a telephone and a writing surface.

In the far back of the room, between the computer table and the whiteboard, is a standard table around which the team meets for CRC sessions. The table is usually covered with CRC cards and food, since one of the team rules is "There must be food."

The room was designed by the team: we actually CHOSE to be here. People speak quietly and the noise level is surprisingly low. But when you need help, you can just raise your voice a tiny bit and get it. You'll get help immediately: Note that the floor has no carpet, which means our chairs can really move!

FIGURE 5. The DaimlerChrysler C3 work area

If you don't have a reasonable place to work, your project won't be successful. The difference between a good space for the team and a bad space for the team is immediate and dramatic.

It was a watershed moment in my development as a consultant when I was asked to review the object-oriented design for a project. I looked at the system and, sure enough, it was a mess. Then I noticed where everyone was sitting. The team was four senior programmers. They each had a corner office on four corners of a medium-sized building. I told them they should move their offices together. I was brought in because of my knowledge of Smalltalk and objects, and the most valuable suggestion I had was that they should rearrange the furniture.

Facilities is a tough job in any case. There are many conflicting constraints. The facilities planner is judged on how little money they spend, and how much flexibility they retain. The people using the facilities want to work closely with the rest of the team. At the same time, though, they need privacy from which to phone for doctor's appointments.

XP wants to err on the side of too much public space. XP is a communal software development discipline. The team members need to be able to see each other, to hear shouted one-off questions, to "accidentally" hear conversations to which they have vital contributions.

XP can strain facilities. Common office layouts don't work well for XP. Putting your computer in a corner, for example, doesn't work, because it is impossible for two people to sit side-by-side and program. Ordinary cubicle wall heights don't work well—walls between cubicles should be half-height or eliminated entirely. At the same time, the team should be separated from other teams.

The best setup is an open bullpen, with little cubbies around the outside of the space. The team members can keep their personal items in these cubbies, go to them to make phone calls, and spend time at them when they don't want to be interrupted. The rest of the team needs to respect the "virtual" privacy of someone sitting in their cubby. Put the biggest, fastest development machines on tables in the middle of the space (cubbies might or might not contain machines). This way, if someone wants to program, they will naturally be drawn to the open, public space. From here everyone can see what is happening, pairs can form easily, and each pair can draw from the energy of the other pairs who are also developing at the same time.

If you can, reserve a little of the nicest space off to one side for a communal space. Put in an espresso maker, couches, some toys, something to draw people there. Often, the most effective way to get unstuck while you are developing is to step away for a moment. If there is a pleasant space to step away to, you are more likely to do it when you need it.

The courage value finds its expression in the XP attitude toward facilities. If the corporate attitude toward facilities is at odds with the team's attitude, the team wins. If the computers are in the wrong place, they are moved. If the partitions are in the way, they are taken down. If the lights are too bright, they are taken out. If the phones are too loud, one day, mysteriously, they are all found to have cotton stuffed in the bells.

I showed up at a bank on the first day and found that we had been given ugly old one-person desks to work at. The desks had two sets of metal drawers on either side of a little slot into which you could just slide your legs. This was clearly not going to work. We looked around until we found an industrial strength screwdriver, then we took off one set of drawers. Now two people could sit side-by-side at each desk.

All this screwing around with the furniture can get you in trouble. The facilities management people can get downright angry to find that someone has been moving desks around without their permission or involvement (never mind that a request for a change can take weeks or months to fulfil). I say, "Too bad." I have software to write, and if getting rid of a partition helps me write that software better, I'm going to do it. If the organization can't stand that much initiative, then I don't want to work there, anyway.

Taking control of the physical environment sends a powerful message to the team. They are not going to let irrational opposing interests in the organization get in the way of success. Taking control of their physical environment is the first step toward taking control of how they work overall.

Facilities are worthy of constant experimentation (the feedback value at work). After all, the organization spent a gazillion dollars for all that flexible office furniture. All that money would be wasted if you didn't flex the furniture a little. What if these two people's cubbies were closer? Farther? What if the integration machine was in the middle? In the corner? Try it. Whatever works, stays. Whatever doesn't is sacrificed to the next experiment.

Chapter 14

Splitting Business and Technical Responsibility

One key to our strategy is to keep technical people focused on technical problems and business people focused on business problems. The project must be driven by business decisions, but the business decisions must be informed by technical decisions about cost and risk.

There are two common failure modes in the relationship between Business and Development. If either Business or Development gains too much power, the project suffers.

Business

If Business has the power, they feel fit to dictate all four variables to Development. "Here is what you will do. Here is when it will be done. No, you can't have any new workstations. And it better be of the highest quality or you're in trouble, buster."

In this scenario, Business always specifies too much. Some of the items on the list of requirements are absolutely essential. But some are not. And if Development doesn't have any power, they can't object; they can't force Business to choose which is which. So Development dutifully goes to work, heads down, on the impossible task they have been given.

It seems to be in the nature of the less important requirements that they entail the greatest risk. They are typically the poorest understood, so there is great risk that the requirements will change all during development. Somehow, they also tend to be technically riskier.

The result of the "Business in Charge" scenario, then, is that the project takes on too much effort and way, way too much risk for too little return.

Development

Now, when Development gets their turn in charge, you would think life would get better. But it doesn't. The net effect is exactly the same.

When Development is in charge, they put in place all the process and technology that they never had time for when "those suits" were pushing them around. They install new tools, new languages, new technologies. And the tools, languages, and technologies are chosen because they are interesting and cutting edge. Cutting edge implies risk. (If we haven't learned that by now, when will we?)

So, the net result of the "Development in Charge" scenario is too much effort and way, way too much risk for too little return.

What to Do?

The solution is to somehow split the responsibility and power between Business and Development. Business people should make the decisions for which they are suited. Programmers should make the decisions for which they are suited. Each party's decisions should inform the other's. Neither party should be able to unilaterally decide anything.

Maintaining this kind of political balancing act might seem well-nigh impossible. If the U.N. can't do it, what chance do you have? Well, if all you had was the vague goal of "balancing political power," you would have no chance. The first strong personality that came along would upset the balance. Fortunately, the goal can be far more concrete than that.

First, a story. If someone asks me whether I want the Ferrari or the minivan, I am almost certain to choose the Ferrari. It will inevitably be more fun. However, as soon as someone says, "Do you want the Ferrari for 200,000 francs or the minivan for 40,000?" I can begin to make an informed decision. Adding new requirements like "I need to be able to carry five kids" or "It has to go 200 kilometers in an hour" clear the picture further. There are cases where either decision makes sense, but you can't possibly make a good decision based only on glossy photographs. You need to know what resources you have, what constraints you have, and how much each one costs.

Following this model, business people should choose

⋄ The scope or timing of releases
⋄ The relative priorities of proposed features
⋄ The exact scope of proposed features

To these decisions the development organization must contribute

⋄ Estimates of the time required to implement various features.
⋄ Estimates of the consequences of various technical alternatives.
⋄ A development process that suits their personalities, their business environment, and their company culture. No single list of "Here's how you write software" can possibly fit every situation. In fact, no single list can possibly fit any situation, since the situation is always in flux.
⋄ What set of practices they will use to begin with, and the process by which they will review the effects of those practices and experiment with changes. This is rather like the U.S. Constitution, which sets out a basic philosophy, a basic set of rules (the Bill of Rights, the first 10 amendments), and rules for changing the rules (adding new amendments).

Since business decisions take place all through the life of a project, giving business people responsibility for business decisions implies that a customer is as much a part of an XP team as a programmer. In particular, for best results they sit with the rest of the team and are available full-time to answer questions.

Choice of Technology

While the choice of a technology might seem at first to be a purely technical decision, it is actually a business decision, but one that must be taken with input from Development. The customer will have to live with a database or language vendor for many years, and has to be comfortable with the relationship at a business level just as much as at a technical level.

If a customer says to me, "We want this system, and you have to use this relational database and that Java IDE," my job is to point out the consequences of that decision. If I think an object database and C++ is a better fit, I'll estimate the project both ways. Then the business people can make a business decision.

There is another side to technology decisions, however, one that lies firmly in the camp of Development. Once a technology has been introduced into a company, someone has to keep it alive as long as it is in use. The costs of the latest and greatest technology are not just in initial production development, or even entirely in development at all. The costs have to include the cost of building and maintaining the competence to keep the technology alive.

What if It's Hard?

Most of the time, the decisions that come out of this process are surprisingly simple to implement. Programmers are good at seeing monsters lurking under every story. The business people say, "I had no idea that was so expensive. Just do this one third of it. That will do fine for now."

Sometimes, though, it doesn't work out that way. Sometimes, the smallest, most valuable chunk of development is large and risky from the programmers' perspective. When this happens, you can't blink. You will have to be careful. You can afford few mistakes. You may have to pull in more outside resources. But when the time comes to go over the top of the trench, then you really earn your money. You do everything you can to encourage smaller scope. You do everything you can think of to reduce risk. But then you just go for it.

Another way of saying this is that the split of power between Business and Development is not an excuse to avoid tough jobs. Quite the contrary. It is a way of sorting out those jobs that are genuinely tough from those jobs that you just haven't figured out how to make simple yet. Most of the time the work will be simpler than you first imagined. When it isn't, you do it anyway, because that is what you get paid for.

Chapter 15

Planning Strategy

We will plan by quickly making an overall plan, then refining it further and further on shorter and shorter time horizons— years, months, weeks, days. We will make the plan quickly and cheaply, so there will be little inertia when we must change it.

Planning is the process of guessing what it will be like to develop a piece of software with a customer. Some of the purposes of planning are to

- ✧ Bring the team together
- ✧ Decide on scope and priorities
- ✧ Estimate cost and schedule
- ✧ Give everyone involved confidence that the system can actually be done
- ✧ Provide a benchmark for feedback

Let's review the principles that affect planning. (Some of them are general principles from Chapter 8, Basic Principles. Others are specific to planning.)

- ✧ Do only the planning you need for the next horizon—At any given level of detail, only plan to the next horizon—that is, the next release, the end of the next iteration. This doesn't mean that you can't do long-range planning. You can, just not in great detail. You can cover this release in great detail and cover the next five (proposed) releases with a set of bullet items. Such a sketch will not lose much over trying to plan all six releases in detail.

✧ Accepted responsibility—Responsibility can only be accepted, not given. This means that there is no such thing as top-down planning in XP. The manager can't go to the team and say, "Here's the pile of stuff we have to do and here's how long it will take." The project manager has to ask the team to take responsibility for doing the work. And then listen to the answer.

✧ The person responsible for implementing gets to estimate—If the team takes responsibility for getting something done, they get to say how long it will take. If an individual on the team takes responsibility for getting something done, they get to say how long it will take.

✧ Ignore dependencies between parts—Plan as if the parts of development can be switched around at will. As long as you are careful to implement the highest business priorities first, this simple rule will keep you from trouble. "How much for the coffee?" "The coffee is 25 cents, but refills are free." "Just give me a refill, then." This doesn't tend to happen.

✧ Planning for priorities vs. planning for development—Be aware of the purposes of planning. Planning so the customer can establish priorities needs much less detail to be valuable than planning for implementation, where you need specific test cases.

The Planning Game

XP planning purposely abstracts the planning process to two participants—Business and Development. This can help to remove some of the unhelpful emotional heat from the discussion of plans. Instead of, "Joe, you idiot, you promised me this by Friday," the Planning Game says, "Development learned something. It needs help from Business in responding in the best way." There is no way that a simple set of rules is going to eliminate emotion, nor is it intended to. The rules are there to remind everyone of how they would like to act, and they provide a common reference when things aren't going well.

Business often doesn't like Development. Relations between the people who need systems and the people who build systems is so strained, they often resemble the relations between centuries-old enemies. Mistrust, accusations, and subtle and indirect maneuvering all abound. You can't develop decent software in this kind of environment.

If this doesn't describe your environment, good for you. The best environment is one of mutual trust. Each party respects the other. Each party believes that the other has their best interest at heart, and the interests of the larger community. Each party is willing to let the other do their job, joining the skills, experience and perspective of both.

You can't legislate this kind of relationship. You can't just say, "We know we've screwed up. We're terribly sorry. It won't happen again. Let's work completely differently, starting right after lunch." The world, and people, just don't work that way. Under stress, people revert to earlier behavior, no matter how badly that behavior has worked in the past.

What is needed on the way to a mutually respectful relationship is a set of rules to govern how the relationship is conducted—who gets to make which decisions, when the decisions will be made, how those decisions will be recorded.

Never forget, however, that the rules of the game are an aid, a step toward the relationship you really want with your customers. The rules can never capture the subtlety, flexibility, and passion of real human relations. Without some set of rules, however, you can't begin to improve the situation. Once the rules are in place and your relationship is improving, then you can begin to modify the rules to make development go more smoothly. Eventually, once they have become habit, you can abandon the rules altogether.

First, however, you have to learn to play by the rules. Here they are.

The Goal

The goal of the game is to maximize the value of software produced by the team. From the value of the software, you have to deduct the cost of its development, and the risk incurred during development.

The Strategy

The strategy for the team is to invest as little as possible to put the most valuable functionality into production as quickly as possible, but only in conjunction with the programming and design strategies designed to reduce risk. In the light of the technology and business lessons of this first system, it becomes clear to Business what is now the most valuable functionality, and the team quickly puts this into production. And so on.

The Pieces

The pieces in the planning game are the story cards. Figure 6 shows an example of one.

The Players

The two players in the Planning Game are Development and Business. Development consists collectively of all the people who will be responsible for implementing the system. Business consists collectively of all the people who will make the decisions about what the system is supposed to do.

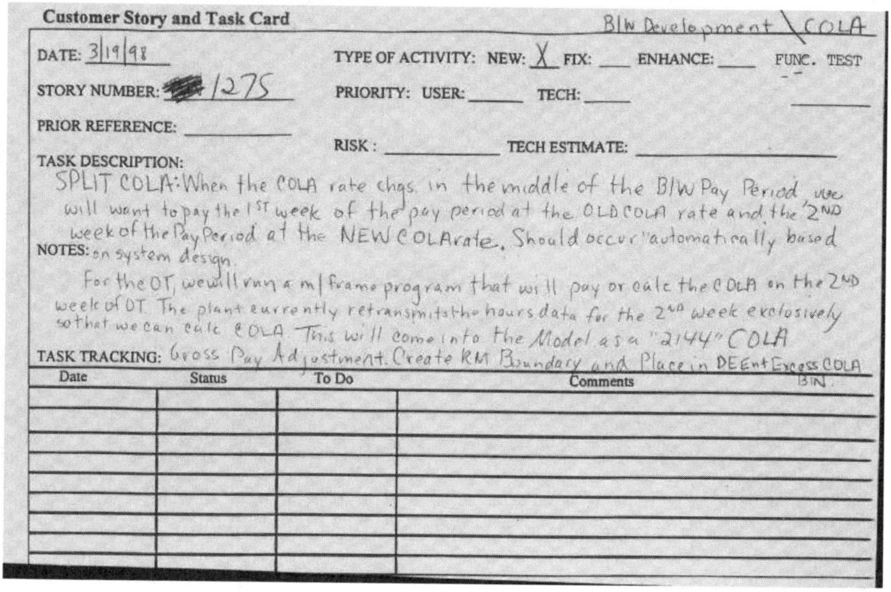

Customer Story and Task Card — B/W Development \ COLA

DATE: 3/19/98 — TYPE OF ACTIVITY: NEW: X FIX: ___ ENHANCE: ___ FUNC. TEST

STORY NUMBER: 1275 — PRIORITY: USER: ___ TECH: ___

PRIOR REFERENCE: ___ — RISK: ___ TECH ESTIMATE: ___

TASK DESCRIPTION:
SPLIT COLA: When the COLA rate chgs. in the middle of the B/W Pay Period we will want to pay the 1ST week of the pay period at the OLD COLA rate and the 2ND week of the Pay Period at the NEW COLA rate. Should occur "automatically based on system design.

NOTES:
For the OT, we will run a m/frame program that will pay or calc the COLA on the 2ND week of OT. The plant currently retransmits the hours data for the 2ND week exclusively so that we can calc COLA. This will come into the Model as a "2144" COLA

TASK TRACKING: Gross Pay Adjustment. Create RM Boundary and Place in DEEnt Excess COLA BIN.

Date	Status	To Do	Comments

FIGURE 6. A story card

Sometimes it's easy to see who plays the part of Business in the Planning Game. If a bond trader is paying for a piece of custom-made software, then they get to be Business. They get to decide what is most important to do first. What if you are building a mass-market shrink-wrap product? Who is Business then? Business needs to make decisions about scope, priority, and the content of releases. These are decisions that are ordinarily made by the marketing department. If they are smart, they will support their decisions by referring to:

- Real users of the product
- Focus groups
- Salespeople

Some of the best players of Business I have seen have been expert users. For example, I worked on a customer service system for a mutual fund. Business was played primarily by a customer service supervisor who had worked her way up after working on the preceding system for years and years, and knew every detail of it. From time to time she had trouble separating what the new system should do from what the old system did, but after a while of working with stories she learned.

The Moves

There are three phases to the game.

- Exploration—Find out what new things the system could do.
- Commitment—Decide what subset of all possible requirements to pursue next.
- Steer—Guide development as reality molds the plan.

The moves from each phase are typically done in that phase, but not strictly. You will write new stories during the steering phase, for example. The phases are also cyclical; after you have been steering for a while you will need to go back to exploration.

Exploration Phase

The purpose of the exploration phase is to give both players an appreciation for what all the system should eventually do. Exploration has three moves.

Write a story—Business writes a story describing something the system needs to do. The stories are written on index cards, with a name and a short paragraph describing the purpose of the story.

Estimate a story—Development estimates how long the story will take to implement. If Development can't estimate the story, it can ask Business to clarify or split the story. A simple method for estimating stories is to ask yourself, "How long would this take me to implement if this story was all I had to implement, and I had no interruptions or meetings?" In XP we call this Ideal Engineering Time. As you will see below (in Set Velocity), before you commit to a schedule you measure a ratio between ideal time and the calendar.

Split a story—If Development can't estimate a whole story, or if Business realizes that part of a story is more important than the rest, Business can split a story into two or more stories.

Commitment Phase

The purpose of the commitment phase is for Business to choose the scope and date of the next release, and for Development to confidently commit to delivering it. The commitment phase has four moves.

Sort by value—Business sorts the stories into three piles: (1) those without which the system will not function, (2) those that are less essential but provide significant business value, and (3) those that would be nice to have.

Sort by risk—Development sorts the stories into three piles: (1) those that they can estimate precisely, (2) those that they can estimate reasonably well, and (3) those that they cannot estimate at all.

Set velocity—Development tells Business how fast the team can program in Ideal Engineering Time per calendar month.

Choose scope—Business chooses the set of cards in the release, either by setting a date for engineering to be complete and choosing cards based on their estimate and the project velocity, or by choosing the cards and calculating the date.

Steering Phase

The purpose of the steering phase is to update the plan based on what is learned by Development and Business. The steering phase has four moves.

Iteration—At the beginning of each iteration (every one to three weeks), Business picks one iteration worth of the most valuable stories to be implemented. The stories for the first iteration must result in a system that runs end-to-end, however embryonically.

Recovery—If Development realizes that it has overestimated its velocity, it can ask Business what is the most valuable set of stories to retain in the current release based on the new velocity and estimates.

New story—If Business realizes it needs a new story during the middle of the development of a release, it can write the story. Development estimates the story, then Business removes stories with the equivalent estimate from the remaining plan and inserts the new story.

Reestimate—If Development feels that the plan no longer provides an accurate map of development, it can reestimate all of the remaining stories and set velocity again.

Iteration Planning

The Planning Game above gives the customer the capability of steering development every three weeks. Within an iteration, the development team applies nearly the same rules to plan their activities.

The Iteration Planning Game is similar to the Planning Game in that cards are used as the pieces. This time, though, the pieces are task cards instead of story cards. The players are all the individual programmers. The time scale is shorter—the whole game plays out in an iteration (one to four weeks). The phases and moves are similar.

Exploration Phase

Write a task—Take the stories for the iteration and turn them into tasks. Generally the tasks are smaller than the whole story, because you can't implement a whole story in a couple of days. Sometimes one task will support several stories. Sometimes a task won't directly relate to any particular story—for example, migrating to a new version of system software. Figure 7 is an example of a real task card.

Engineering Task Card

DATE: 3/17/98

BIN   Based on Conversation w/ REB:RMA

Smalltalk/Future

NEW

STORY NUMBER: X923   SOFTWARE ENGINEER: _____   TASK ESTIMATE: _____

TASK DESCRIPTION:

Composite Bin — Regular Base Needs to Be Displayed on GUI. We have the hidden bin for Regular Base (Lost Time) to display NOT the auto gen bin but the BIN that composites the Auto Pay + the Lost Time. There is

SOFTWARE ENGINEER'S NOTES: a separate composite bin started that needs to be completed??

TASK TRACKING:

Date	Done	To Do	Comments

FIGURE 7. A task card

Split a task/combine tasks—If you can't estimate a task at a few days, break it down into smaller tasks. If several tasks each take an hour, combine them to form a larger task.

Commitment Phase

Accept a task—A programmer accepts responsibility for a task.

Estimate a task—The responsible programmer estimates the number of ideal engineering days to implement each task. Often this is conditional on getting help from another programmer who may be more familiar with code to be modified. Tasks that take more than a few days must be split (you'll have to discover the exact threshold for yourself by comparing tasks that came in on time with tasks that didn't).

You might think you would have to explicitly factor in the effects of pair programming in your estimates. Ignore it. The time you spend helping other programmers, talking with the customer, and going to meetings shows up in the load factor.

Set load factors—Each programmer chooses their load factor for the iteration—the percentage of time they will spend actually developing. This is a measured number—the relationship of ideal programming days to the calendar. If for the last three iterations you've completed 6, 8, and 7.5 ideal days worth of tasks, then that's about what you should sign up for this iteration. The number of ideal days of tasks per iteration can be quite low for newer team members or a coach—2 or 3 days in a three week iteration. It shouldn't be higher than 7 or 8 for anyone, or they won't spend enough time helping.

Balancing—Each programmer adds up their task estimates and multiplies by their load factor. Programmers who turn out to be overcommitted must give up some tasks. If the whole team is overcommitted, they must find a way to get back on balance (see Recovery, below).

Steering Phase

Implement a task—A programmer takes a task card, finds a partner, writes the test cases for the task, makes them all work, then integrates and releases the new code when the universal test suite runs.

Record progress—Every two or three days one member of the team asks each programmer how long they have spent on each of their tasks and how many days they have left.

Recovery—Programmers who turn out to be overcommitted ask for help by (1) reducing the scope of some tasks, (2) asking the customer to reduce the scope of some stories, (3) shedding nonessential tasks, (4) getting more or better help, and as a last resort (5) asking the customer to defer some stories to a later iteration.

Verify story—As soon as the functional tests are ready and the tasks for a story are complete, the functional tests are run to verify that the story works. Interesting cases brought to life during implementation can be added to the functional test suite.

The differences between iteration planning and release planning are primarily that you can tolerate more wiggling in the iteration schedule than in the commitment schedule. If one of three weeks has passed in an iteration and progress has been too slow, it is entirely possible to stop for a day for a major collaborative refactoring that is needed for everyone's progress. No programmer is going to get the feeling that the whole project is falling apart at that point (not after a little experience). If the customer saw such seemingly drastic changes on a daily basis, however, they would quickly become nervous.

In a way this seems like lying, because you are concealing some of the process of development from the customer. It is important that this doesn't become true. You don't deliberately conceal anything. If the customer wants to sit through a whole day of refactoring, well, they probably have more valuable things to do, but they are certainly welcome. The distinction between inter- and intra-iteration planning is an extension to the principle of splitting business and technical decisions. There are changes at a certain level of detail that are no longer the concern of Business—programmers know how to micromanage their time better than any business person could.

One difference between the Planning Game and the Iteration Planning Game is that programmers sign up for the tasks before they estimate. The team implicitly takes collective responsibility for the stories, so the estimates should be made by the team collectively. Individual programmers accept responsibilities for tasks, so they must estimate the tasks themselves.

Another difference with iteration planning is that some of the tasks are not directly related to the needs of the customer. If someone needs to strengthen the tools for integration, and it is enough work that it can't easily be hidden in the cracks of development, then it becomes a task of its own, scheduled and prioritized with all the other tasks.

Let's look back at the constraints on the iteration planning process and how the strategy above meets them.

⋄ You don't want to spend too much time planning, since reality will never consent to match the plan exactly. Half a day out of fifteen is not so much overhead. Of course, if you could reduce that time it would be better, but it is not so much time.

⋄ You want rapid feedback on how you are doing, so a third of the way through you will know whether you are in trouble. The answers to the questions the person tracking progress asks give you a fair idea halfway through the iteration if you are on schedule or not. That is often enough time to react locally to problems, without asking the customer to make changes.

- You want the individuals responsible for delivering something to also be responsible for estimating it. As long as the programmers sign up for tasks before they estimate, this works.
- You want to limit the scope of development to what is really needed. It always feels strange to say that you can only do 7.5 days of work in three weeks (15 days divided by a measured load factor of 2). However, as your estimates get better and better, you will find that it is absolutely true. That feeling that you aren't really working so terribly hard makes you want to do more tasks. But you know you want to maintain standards and quality as you do so (and you have a partner looking at the same screen to make sure you do maintain quality). So you have a tendency to work simply and still honestly be able to say you've completed the task.
- You want a process that doesn't generate so much pressure that people do things that turn out to be stupid, just to meet the needs of a short-term plan. Again, this goes back to saying that you can do 7.5 days of work. You just can't take on too many tasks. If you do one iteration, there will be ample, public feedback that you shouldn't have tried to do so much. So you won't do it again. This results in your committing to do about as much as you can actually do, with quality.

On smaller projects, I have eliminated iteration planning. It is certainly necessary for coordinating the work of ten programmers. It is certainly not necessary for coordinating the work of two. Depending on the project, you will find that the need to coordinate makes the extra effort involved in formal iteration planning worth it.

Planning in a Week

How can you plan a project if you only have a week? This is a situation that comes up often for teams making fixed-price bids. You receive a tender and you have a week to respond. You don't have enough time to write a complete set of stories, each of which you can estimate and test. You don't have time to write prototypes so you can estimate the stories from experience.

The XP solution is to accept more risk in the plan by having bigger stories. Write stories you can estimate in terms of ideal programming months instead of ideal programming weeks. You can give the customer the opportunity to make tradeoffs by shrinking or deferring some stories, just as you would in the regular Planning Game.

Estimates should be based on experience. Unlike the Planning Game, by responding to a proposal in a week you don't have time to create much experience. You should be estimating from previous experience writing similar systems. If you don't have previous experience writing similar systems, you have no business responding to a fixed-price tender.

Once you are awarded the contract, the first thing you should do is go back and play the opening stages of the Planning Game, so you have an immediate crosscheck on your ability to deliver on the contract.

Chapter 16

Development Strategy

Unlike the management strategy, the development strategy is a radical departure from conventional wisdom—we will carefully craft a solution for today's problem today, and trust that we will be able to solve tomorrow's problem tomorrow.

XP uses the metaphor of programming for its activities—that is, everything you do looks in some way like programming: Programming in XP is like programming, with a few small things added, like automated testing. However, like all the rest of XP, XP development is deceptively simple. All the pieces are simple enough to explain, but executing them is hard. Fear intrudes. Under pressure, old habits return.

The development strategy begins with iteration planning. Continuous integration reduces development conflicts and creates a natural end to a development episode. Collective ownership encourages the whole team to make the whole system better. Finally, pair programming ties the whole process together.

Continuous Integration

No code sits unintegrated for more than a couple of hours. At the end of every development episode, the code is integrated with the latest release and all the tests must run at 100%.

At the outer limit of continuous integration, every time you changed a method, the change would instantly be reflected in everyone else's code. Aside from the infrastructure and bandwidth required to support such a style, this wouldn't work well. While you are developing, you want to pretend that you are the only programmer on the project. You want to march ahead at full speed, ignoring the relationship of the changes you make to the changes anyone else happens to be making. Having changes happen out of your immediate control would shatter this illusion.

Integrating after a few hours (certainly no more than a day) gives many of the benefits of both styles—single programmer and instantaneous integration. While you are developing, you can act like you and your partner are the only pair on the project. You can make changes wherever you want to. Then you switch hats. As integrators, you become aware (the tools tell you) where there are collisions in the definition of classes or methods. By running the tests you become aware of semantic collisions.

If integration took a couple of hours, it would not be possible to work in this style. It is important to have tools that support a fast integration/build/test cycle. You also need a reasonably complete test suite that runs in a few minutes. The effort needed to fix collisions can't be too great.

This isn't a problem. Constant refactoring has the effect of breaking the system into lots of little objects and lots of little methods. This lowers the chance that two pairs of programmers will change the same class or method at the same time. If they do, the effort required to reconcile the changes is small, because each only represents a few hours of development.

Another important reason to accept the costs of continuous integration is that it dramatically reduces the risk of the project. If two people have different ideas about the appearance or operation of a piece of code, you will know in hours. You will never spend days chasing a bug that was created some time in the last few weeks. And all that practice at integration comes in very handy when it comes to creating the final project. The "production build" is no big deal. Everyone on the team could do it in their sleep by the time it comes around, because they have been doing it every day for months.

Continuous integration also provides a valuable human benefit during development. In the middle of working on a task you have a hundred things on your mind. By working until there is a natural break—there are no more small items on the to-do card—and then integrating, you provide a rhythm to development. Learn/test/code/release. It's almost like breathing. You form an idea, you express it, you add it to the system. Now your mind is clear, ready for the next idea.

From time to time, continuous integration forces you to split the implementation of a task into two episodes. We accept the overhead this causes, the need to remember what was done already and what remains to be done. In the interim, you may have an insight into what caused the first episode to go so slowly. You start the next episode with some refactoring, and the rest of the second episode goes much more smoothly.

Collective Ownership

Collective ownership is this seemingly crazy idea that anyone can change any piece of code in the system at any time. Without the tests, you'd simply be dead trying to do this. With the tests, and the quality of tests you get after a few months of writing lots of tests, you can get away with this. You can get away with this if you only integrate a few hours worth of changes at a time. Which, of course, is exactly what you will do.

One of the effects of collective ownership is that complex code does not live very long. Because everyone is used to looking all over the system, such code will be found sooner rather than later. And when it is found, someone will try to simplify it. If the simplification doesn't work, as evidenced by the tests failing, then the code will be thrown away. Even if this happens, there will be someone other than the original pair who understands why the code might have to be complex. More often than not, however, the simplification works, or at least part of it works.

Collective ownership tends to prevent complex code from entering the system in the first place. If you know that someone else will soon (in a few hours) be looking at what you are writing at the moment, you will think twice before putting in a complexity you can't immediately justify.

Collective ownership increases your feeling of personal power on a project. On an XP project you are never stuck with someone else's stupidity. You see something in the way, you get it out of the way. If you choose to live with something for the moment because it is expedient, that is your business. But you're never stuck. So you never get the sense that, "I could get my work done, if only I didn't have to deal with these other idiots." One less frustration. One step closer to clear thinking.

Collective ownership also tends to spread knowledge of the system around the team. It is unlikely that there will ever be a part of the system that only two people know (it has to be at least a pair, which is already better than the usual situation where one smart programmer holds everyone else hostage). This further reduces project risk.

Pair Programming

Pair programming really deserves its own book. It is a subtle skill, one that you can spend the rest of your life getting good at. For the purposes of this chapter, we'll just look at why it works for XP.

First, a couple of words about what pair programming isn't. It isn't one person programming while another person watches. Just watching someone program is about as interesting as watching grass die in a desert. Pair programming is a dialog between two people trying to simultaneously program (and analyze and design and test) and understand together how to program better. It is a conversation at many levels, assisted by and focused on a computer.

Pair programming is also not a tutoring session. Sometimes pairs contain one partner with much more experience than the other partner. When this is true, the first few sessions will look a lot like tutoring. The junior partner will ask lots of questions, and type very little. Very quickly, though, the junior partner will start catching stupid little mistakes, like unbalanced parentheses. The senior partner will notice the help. After a few more weeks, the junior partner will start picking up the larger patterns that the senior partner is using, and notice deviations from those patterns.

In a couple of months, typically, the gap between the partners is not nearly so noticeable as it was at first. The junior partner is typing more regularly. The pair notices that each of them has strengths and weaknesses. Productivity, quality, and satisfaction rise.

Pair programming is not about being joined at the hip. If you look at Chapter 2, A Development Episode, you will notice that the first thing I did was ask for help. Sometimes you are looking for a particular partner when you start a task. More commonly, though, you just find someone who is available. And, if you both have tasks to do, you agree to work the morning on one task and the afternoon on the other.

What if two people just don't get along? They don't have to pair. Two people who can't pair make arranging the rest of the pairings more awkward. If the interpersonal problem is bad enough, a few moments shuffling pairs is better than a fist fight.

What if someone refuses to pair? They can choose to learn to work like the rest of the team, or they can choose to look for work outside of the team. XP is not for everybody, and not everybody is for XP. You don't have to start pairing full-time the first day you work extreme, however. Like everything else, you have to work toward it a little at a time. Try it for an hour. If it doesn't work, try to figure out what went wrong and try it again for an hour.

So, why does pair programming work for XP? Well, the first value is communication, and there are few forms of communication more intense than face-to-face. So, pair programming works for XP because it encourages communication. I like to think of the analogy of a pool of water. When an important new bit of information is learned by someone on the team, it is like putting a drop of dye in the water. Because of the pairs switching around all the time, the information rapidly diffuses throughout the team just as the dye spreads throughout the pool. Unlike the dye, however, the information becomes richer and more intense as it spreads and is enriched by the experience and insight of everyone on the team.

In my experience, pair programming is more productive than dividing the work between two programmers and then integrating the results. Pair programming is often a sticking point for folks wanting to adopt XP. All I can say is that you should get good at it, then try an iteration where you pair for all production code and another where you program everything solo. Then you can make your own decision.

Even if you weren't more productive, you would still want to pair, because the resulting code quality is so much higher. While one partner is busy typing, the other partner is thinking at a more strategic level. Where is this line of development going? Will it run into a dead end? Is there a better overall strategy? Is there an opportunity to refactor?

Another powerful feature of pair programming is that some of the practices wouldn't work without it. Under stress, people revert. They will skip writing tests. They will put off refactoring. They will avoid integrating. With your partner watching, though, chances are that even if you feel like blowing off one of these practices, your partner won't. This is not to say that pairs don't ever make process mistakes. They certainly do, or you wouldn't need the coach. But the chances of ignoring your commitment to the rest of the team is much smaller in pairs than it is when you are working alone.

The conversational nature of pair programming also enhances the software development process. You quickly learn to talk at many different levels—this code here, code like this elsewhere in the system, development episodes like this in the past, systems like this from years past, the practices you are using and how they can be made better.

Chapter 17

Design Strategy

We will continually refine the design of the system, starting from a very simple beginning. We will remove any flexibility that doesn't prove useful.

In many ways, this is the most difficult chapter to write. The design strategy in XP is to always have the simplest design that runs the current test suite.

Now, that didn't hurt so bad. What's wrong with simplicity? What's wrong with test suites?

The Simplest Thing That Could Possibly Work

Let's take a step back and come on this answer a little at a time. All four values play into this strategy:

◈ *Communication*—A complicated design is harder to communicate than a simple one. We should therefore create a design strategy that comes up with the simplest possible design, consistent with the rest of our goals. On the other hand, we should create a design strategy that comes up with communicative designs, where the elements of the design communicate important aspects of the system to a reader.

◈ *Simplicity*—We should have a design strategy that will produce simple designs, but the strategy itself should be simple. This doesn't mean that it needs to be easy to execute. Good design is never easy. But the expression of the strategy should be simple.

✧ *Feedback*—One of the problems I always had designing before I began practicing XP was that I didn't know when I was right or wrong. The longer I went on designing, the worse this problem became. A simple design solves this by being done quickly. The next thing to do is code it and see how the code appears.

✧ *Courage*—What could be more courageous than stopping after a little bit of design, confident that when the time comes, you can add more, when and as needed?

Following these values, we have to:

✧ Create a design strategy that results in a design that is simple.

✧ Quickly find a way to verify its quality.

✧ Feed back what we learn into the design.

✧ Crank the cycle time for this whole process down as short as possible.

The principles also work into the design strategy.

✧ *Small initial investment*—We should make the smallest possible investment in the design before getting payback for it.

✧ *Assume simplicity*—We should assume that the simplest design we can imagine possibly working actually will work. This will give us time to do a thorough job in case the simplest design doesn't work. In the meantime, we won't have to carry along the cost of extra complexity.

✧ *Incremental change*—The design strategy will work by gradual change. We will design a little at a time. There will never be a time when the system "is designed." It will always be subject to change, although there will be parts of the system that remain quiet for a while.

✧ *Travel light*—The design strategy should produce no "extra" design. There should be enough to suit our current purposes (the need to do quality work), but no more. If we embrace change, we will be willing to start simple and continually refine.

XP works against many programmers' instincts. As programmers, we get in the habit of anticipating problems. When they appear later, we're happy. When they don't appear, we don't notice. So the design strategy will have to go sideways of this "guessing at the future" behavior. Fortunately, most folks can unlearn the habit of "borrowing trouble" (as my grandmother called it). Unfortunately, the smarter you are, the harder it will be to unlearn.

Another way of looking at this is by asking the question, "When do you add more design?" A common answer is that you should design for tomorrow, as shown in Figure 8.

This strategy works if nothing changes between now and later. If you know exactly what is going to happen, and you know exactly how to solve it, it is generally better to add what you need now, and add what you need later, too.

The problem with this strategy is uncertainty. In particular,

⬦ Sometimes tomorrow never comes (that is, the feature you designed ahead for is taken off your plate by the customer).
⬦ Sometimes you learn a better way to work between now and later.

In either case, you then must choose between paying the cost of taking out the excess design or paying the ongoing cost of carrying along a more complicated design that brings no current benefit.

I never want to bet against change happening, and I certainly don't want to bet against the possibility that I am going to learn. In that case, we need to change the picture to reflect that we will design for today's

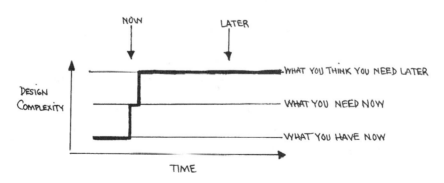

FIGURE 8. **If the cost of change grows dramatically over time**

problems today, and tomorrow's problems tomorrow, as shown in Figure 10.

This leads us to the following design strategy.

1. Start with a test, so we will know when we are done. We have to do a certain amount of design just to write the test: What are the objects and their visible methods?
2. Design and implement just enough to get that test running. You will have to design enough of the implementation to get this test and all previous tests running.
3. Repeat.
4. If you ever see the chance to make the design simpler, do it. See the subsection What Is Simplest? for a definition of the principles that drive this.

This strategy may look ridiculously simple. It is simple. It is not ridiculous. It is capable of creating large, sophisticated systems. However, it is not easy. Nothing is harder than working under a tight deadline and still taking the time to clean up as you go.

Designing in this style, you will implement something in a very simple way the first time you encounter it. The second time you use it, you will make it more general. The first use only pays what it must. The second use pays for flexibility. This way you never pay for flexibility you don't use, and you tend to make the system flexible where it needs to be flexible for the third, fourth, and fifth variations.

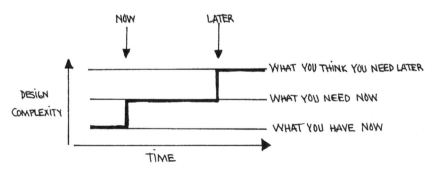

FIGURE 10. **If change remains cheap over time**

How Does "Designing Through Refactoring" Work?

It's in execution that the design strategy will feel strange. We'll pick up the first test case. We'll say, "If all we had to do was implement this test case, then we would only need one object with two methods." We'll implement the object and the two methods. And we'll be done. Our whole design is one object. For about a minute.

Then we'll pick up the next test case. Well, we could just hack in a solution, or we could restructure the existing one object into two objects. Then implementing the test case would involve replacing one of the objects. So, we restructure first, run the first test case to make sure it works, then implement the next test case.

After a day or two of this, the system is big enough that we can imagine two teams working on it without worrying about stepping on each other all the time. So we get two pairs implementing test cases at the same time and periodically (a few hours at a time) integrating their changes. Another day or two and the system can support the whole team developing in this style.

From time to time, the team will get the feeling that the crud has been creeping up behind them. Perhaps they have measured a consistent deviation from their estimates. Or maybe their stomachs knot up when they know they have to change a certain part of the system. In any case, somebody calls, "Time out." The team gets together for a day and restructures the system as a whole using a combination of CRC cards, sketches, and refactoring.

Not all refactorings can be accomplished in a few minutes. If you discover that you have built a big tangled inheritance hierarchy, it might take a month of concentrated effort to untangle it. But you don't have a month of concentrated effort to spend. You have to deliver stories for this iteration.

When faced with a big refactoring, you have to take it in small steps (incremental change again). You'll be in the middle of a test case, and you'll see a chance to take one more step toward your big goal. Take that one step. Move a method here, a variable there. Eventually all that will remain of the big refactoring is a little job. Then you can finish it in a few minutes.

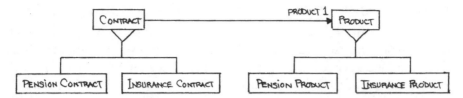

FIGURE 11. UML for Contract with subclasses for Insurance Contract and Pension Contract referring to a Product with subclasses Insurance Product and Pension Product

I experienced taking large-scale refactorings a step at a time on an insurance contract management system. We had the hierarchy as shown in Figure 10.

This design violates the Once and Only Once rule. So we began working on moving to a design like that shown in Figure 11.

In the year I spent on this system we made many small steps toward our desired design. We pushed responsibility in the Contract subclasses either into the Function or the Product subclasses. At the end of my contract we still hadn't eliminated the Contract subclasses, but they were much slimmer than at the beginning, and they were clearly on their way out. And in the meantime we kept putting new functionality into production.

And that's it. That's how you design extreme. In the XP view, design is not drawing a bunch of pictures and then implementing the system to conform to the pictures. That would be pointing the car. Learning to Drive points the way to a different style of design—get the car started, then point it a little this way, then a little that way, then this way again.

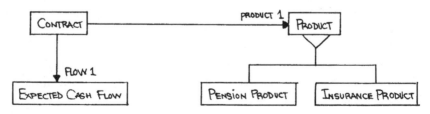

FIGURE 12. Contract refers to a Function but has no subclasses

What Is Simplest?

So, the definition of the best design is the simplest design that runs all the test cases. The effectiveness of this definition turns on, what do we mean by simplest?

Is the simplest design the one with the fewest classes? This would lead to objects that were too big to be effective. Is the simplest design the one with the fewest methods? This would lead to big methods and duplication. Is the simplest design the one with the fewest lines of code? This would lead to compression for compression's sake and a loss of communication.

Here is what I mean by simplest—four constraints, in priority order.

1. The system (code and tests together) must communicate everything you want to communicate.
2. The system must contain no duplicate code. (1 and 2 together constitute the Once and Only Once rule).
3. The system should have the fewest possible classes.
4. The system should have the fewest possible methods.

The purpose of the design of the system is, first, to communicate the intent of the programmers and, second, to provide a place for the logic of the system to live. The constraints above provide a framework within which to satisfy these two requirements.

If you view the design as a communication medium, then you will have objects or methods for every important concept. You will choose the names of classes and methods to work together.

Constrained as you are to communicate, then you must find a way to eliminate all the duplicated logic in the system. This is the hardest part of design for me, because you first have to find the duplication, and then you have to find a way to eliminate it. Eliminating duplication naturally leads you to create lots of little objects and lots of little methods, because otherwise there will inevitably be duplication.

But you don't just create new objects or methods for the fun of it. If you ever find yourself with a class that does nothing and communicates nothing or a method that does nothing and communicates nothing, then you delete it.

Another way of looking at this process is as erasure. You have a system that runs the test cases. You delete everything that doesn't have a purpose—either a communication purpose or a computational purpose. What you are left with is the simplest design that could possibly work.

How Could This Work?

The traditional strategy for reducing the cost of software over time is to reduce the probability and cost of rework. XP goes exactly backwards. Rather than reduce the frequency of rework, XP revels in rework. A day without refactoring is like a day without sunshine. How could this possibly cost less?

The key is that risk is money just as much as time is money. If you put in a design feature today and you use it tomorrow, you win, because you pay less to put it in today. Chapter 3, Economics of Software Development, however, suggests that this evaluation is not complete. If there is enough uncertainty, the value of the option of waiting is high enough that you would be better off waiting.

Design isn't free. Another aspect of this situation is that when you put more design in today, you increase the overhead of the system. There is more to test, more to understand, more to explain. So every day you don't just pay interest on the money you spent, you also pay a little design tax. With this in mind, the difference in today's investment and tomorrow's investment can be much greater and it is still a good idea to design tomorrow for tomorrow's problems.

As if this weren't enough, the killer is risk. As the Economics of Software Development pointed out, you can't just evaluate the cost of something that happens tomorrow. You also have to evaluate the probability of it happening. Now, I love to guess and be right just as much as anybody, but what I discovered when I started paying attention was that I didn't guess right nearly as often as I thought. Often the fabulous design that I created a year ago had nearly no correct guesses. I had to rework every bit of the design before I was done, sometimes two or three times.

So, the cost of making a design decision today is the cost of making the decision plus the interest we pay on that money plus the inertia it adds to the system. The benefit of making a design decision today is the expected value of the decision being profitably used in the future.

If the cost of today's decision is high, and the probability of its being right is low, and the probability of knowing a better way tomorrow is high, and the cost of putting in the design tomorrow is low, then we can conclude that we should never make a design decision today if we don't need it today. In fact, that is what XP concludes. "Sufficient to the day are the troubles thereof."

Now, several factors can make the above evaluation null and void. If the cost of making the change tomorrow is very much higher, then we should make the decision today on the off chance that we are right. If the inertia of the design is low enough (for example, you have really, really smart people), then the benefits of just-in-time design are less. If you are a really, really good guesser, then you could go ahead and design everything today. For the rest of us, however, I don't see any alternative to the conclusion that today's design should be done today and tomorrow's design should be done tomorrow.

Role of Pictures in Design

But what about all those pretty pictures of designs and analyses? Some people really do think better about their designs in terms of pictures instead of code. How does a visually oriented person make their contribution to the design?

First, there is nothing wrong with designing software using explicit pictures instead of a purely mental or textual model of the system, and there is much to be said for a graphical approach. Trouble drawing the pictures can give you subtle clues about the health of a design. If you find it impossible to reduce the number of elements in the picture to manageable levels; if there is an obvious asymmetry; if there are many more lines than there are boxes. All of these are clues to a bad design that become evident from a graphical representation of the design.

Another strength of designing with pictures is speed. In the time it would take you to code one design, you can compare and contrast three designs using pictures.

The trouble with pictures, however, is that they can't give you concrete feedback. They give you certain kinds of feedback about the design, but they insulate you from others. Unfortunately, the feedback they insulate you from is exactly the feedback that teaches you the most—Will this run the test cases? Does this support simple code? This is feedback you can get only from coding.

So, on the one hand, we can go fast when we design with pictures. On the other hand, we are at risk when we design with pictures. We need a strategy that let's us take advantage of the strength of designing with pictures that also reduces its weaknesses.

But we are not alone. We have the principles to guide us. Let's see.

- *Small initial investment*—suggests that we draw a few pictures at a time.
- *Play to win*—suggests that we don't use pictures out of fear (for example, because we want to put off the day we admit we don't know what the design should be).
- *Rapid feedback*—suggests that we quickly find out if our pictures are on target or not.
- *Working with people's instincts*—suggests that we encourage pictures from those who work best with pictures.
- *Embracing change and travel light*—suggest that we don't save the pictures once they have had their effect on the code, since the decisions they represent will probably change tomorrow anyway.

The XP strategy is that anyone can design with pictures all they want, but as soon as a question is raised that can be answered with code, the designers must turn to code for the answer. The pictures aren't saved. For example, the pictures could be drawn on a whiteboard. Wishing you could save the whiteboard is a sure sign the design hasn't been communicated, either to the team or to the system.

If there is a kind of source code that is best expressed as pictures, then you should definitely express it, edit it, and maintain it as picture. CASE tools that let you specify the entire behavior of a system are fine. They may call what they do "code generation," but it certainly looks like a programming language to me. My objection is not to pictures, but to trying to keep multiple forms of the same information synchronized.

If you were using a textual programming language, following this advice, you would never spend more than 10 to 15 minutes drawing pictures. Then you know what question you want to ask of the system.

After you get the answer, you can draw a few more pictures, until you reach another question that needs a concrete answer.

The same advice applies to other noncode design notations, like CRC cards. Do a few minutes of it, enough to illuminate a question, then turn to the system to reduce the risk that you have been fooling yourself.

System Architecture

I haven't used the "A" word anywhere above. Architecture is just as important in XP projects as it is in any software project. Part of the architecture is captured by the system metaphor. If you have a good metaphor in place, everyone on the team can tell about how the system as a whole works.

The next step is to see how the story turns into objects. The rules of the Planning Game state that the result of the first iteration must be a functioning skeleton of the system as a whole. But you still have to do the simplest thing that could possibly work. How can you reconcile these two?

For the first iteration, pick a set of simple, basic stories that you expect will force you to create the whole architecture. Then narrow your horizon and implement the stories in the simplest way that can possibly work. At the end of this exercise you will have your architecture. It may not be the architecture you expected, but then you will have learned something.

What if you can't find a set of stories that forces you to create the architecture you know, you absolutely know, you are going to need? Either you can put the whole architecture in place on speculation, or you can put as much architecture in place now as you need to meet your current needs, and trust that you can put more in later. I put in the architecture I need now and trust my ability to change it later.

Chapter 18

Testing Strategy

We will write tests before we code, minute by minute. We will preserve these tests forever, and run them all together frequently. We will also derive tests from the customer's perspective.

Oh yuck. Nobody wants to talk about testing. Testing is the ugly stepchild of software development. The problem is, everybody knows that testing is important. Everybody knows they don't do enough testing. And we feel it—our projects don't go as well as they should and we feel like more testing might help the problem. But then we read a testing book and instantly get bogged down in the many kinds and ways of testing. There's no way we could do all that and still get any development done.

Here's what XP testing is like. Every time a programmer writes some code, they think it is going to work. So every time they think some code is going to work, they take that confidence out of the ether and turn it into an artifact that goes into the program. The confidence is there for their own use. And because it is there in the program, everyone else can use that confidence, too.

The same story works for the customer. Every time they think of something concrete the program should do, they turn it into another piece of confidence that goes into the program. Now their confidence is in there with the programmers' confidence. The program just gets more and more confident.

Now, a testing person would look at XP testing and snicker. This is not the work of someone who loves testing. Quite the contrary. This is the work of someone who loves getting programs working. So you should write the tests that help get programs working and keep programs working. Nothing more.

Remember the principle "Work with human nature, not against it." That is the fundamental mistake in the testing books I've read. They start with the premise that testing is at the center of development. You must do this test and that test and oh yes this other one, too. If we want programmers and customers to write tests, we had better make the process as painless as possible, realizing that the tests are there as instrumentation, and it is the behavior of the system being instrumented that everyone cares about, not the tests themselves. If it was possible to develop without tests, we would dump all the tests in a minute.

Massimo Arnoldi writes:

> *Unfortunately at least for me (and not only) testing goes against human nature. If you release the pig in you, you will see that you program without tests. Then after a while, when your rational part wins, you stop and you start writing tests. You mentioned too, pair programming reduces the probability that both partners are releasing their pigs at the same moment.*
> (Source: e-mail.)

The tests that you must write in XP are isolated and automatic.

First, each test doesn't interact with the others you write. That way you avoid the problem that one test fails and causes a hundred other failures. Nothing discourages testing more than false negatives. You get this adrenaline rush when you arrive in the morning and find a pile of defects. When it turns out to be no big deal, it's a big letdown. Are you going to pay careful attention to the tests after this has happened five or ten times? No way.

The tests are also automatic. Tests are most valuable when the stress level rises, when people are working too much, when human judgment starts to fail. So the tests must be automatic—returning an unqualified thumbs up/thumbs down indication of whether the system is behaving.

It is impossible to test absolutely everything, without the tests being as complicated and error-prone as the code. It is suicide to test nothing (in this sense of isolated, automatic tests). So, of all the things you can imagine testing, what should you test?

You should test things that might break. If code is so simple that it can't possibly break, and you measure that the code in question doesn't actually break in practice, then you shouldn't write a test for it. If I told you to test absolutely everything, pretty soon you would realize that most of the tests you were writing were valueless, and, if you were at all like me, you would stop writing them. "This testing stuff is for the birds."

Testing is a bet. The bet pays off when your expectations are violated. One way a test can pay off is when a test works that you didn't expect to work. Then you better go find out why it works, because the code is smarter than you are. Another way a test can pay off is when a test breaks when you expected it to work. In either case, you learn something. And software development is learning. The more you learn, the better you develop.

So, if you could, you would only write those tests that pay off. Since you can't know which tests would pay off (if you did, then you would already know and you wouldn't be learning anything), you write tests that might pay off. As you test, you reflect on which kinds of tests tend to pay off and which don't, and you write more of the ones that do pay off, and fewer of the ones that don't.

Who Writes Tests?

As I said at the beginning of the chapter, the tests come from two sources:

✧ Programmers
✧ Customers

The programmers write tests method-by-method. A programmer writes a test under the following circumstances.

✧ If the interface for a method is at all unclear, you write a test before you write the method.
✧ If the interface is clear, but you imagine that the implementation will be the least bit complicated, you write a test before you write the method.

✧ If you think of an unusual circumstance in which the code should work as written, you write a test to communicate the circumstance.

✧ If you find a problem later, you write a test that isolates the problem.

✧ If you are about to refactor some code, and you aren't sure how it's supposed to behave, and there isn't already a test for the aspect of the behavior in question, you write a test first.

The programmer-written unit tests always run at 100%. If one of the unit tests is broken, no one on the team has a more important job than fixing the tests. Because, if a test is broken, you have an unknown amount of work to do to fix it. It might only take a minute. But it might take a month. You don't know. And because the programmers control the writing and execution of the unit tests, they can keep the tests completely in sync.

The customers write tests story-by-story. The question they need to ask themselves is, "What would have to be checked before I would be confident that this story was done?" Each scenario they come up with turns into a test, in this case a functional test.

The functional tests don't necessarily run at 100% all of the time. Because they come from a different source than the code itself, I haven't figured out a way to synchronize the tests and the code in the same way that the code and the unit tests are synchronized. So, while the measure of the unit tests is binary—100% or bust—the measure of functional tests is by necessity based on percentages. Over time you expect the functional test scores to rise to near 100%. As you get close to a release, the customer will need to categorize the failing functional tests. Some will be more important to fix than others.

Customers typically can't write functional tests by themselves. They need the help of someone who can first translate their test data into tests, and over time can create tools that let the customers write, run, and maintain their own tests. That's why an XP team of any size carries at least one dedicated tester. The tester's job is to translate the sometimes vague testing ideas of the customer into real, automatic, isolated tests. The tester also uses the customer-inspired tests as the starting point for variations that are likely to break the software.

Even if you have a dedicated tester, someone whose joy comes from breaking software that is supposed to be done already, they work within the same economic framework as programmers writing tests. The tester is placing bets, hoping for a test that succeeds when it should fail or that fails when it should succeed. So the tester is also learning to write better and better tests over time, tests that are more likely to pay off. The tester is certainly not there to just churn out as many tests as possible.

Other Tests

While the unit and functional tests are the heart of the XP testing strategy, there are other tests that may make sense from time to time. An XP team will recognize when they are going astray and a new kind of test could help. They might write any of the following kinds of tests (or any of the other tests you can find in a testing book).

- *Parallel test*—a test designed to prove that the new system works exactly like the old system. Rather, the test shows how the new system differs from the old system, so a business person can make the business decision of when the difference is small enough that they can put the new system into production.
- *Stress test*—a test design to simulate the worst possible load. Stress tests are good for complex systems where the performance characteristics are not easily predictable.
- *Monkey test*—a test designed to make sure the system acts sensibly in the face of nonsensical input.

Section 3

Implementing XP

In this section we will discuss putting the strategies from the last section into practice. Once you choose a radically simplified set of strategies you suddenly have much more flexibility to play with. You can use this flexibility for many purposes, but you need to be aware that it exists and what possibilities it opens up for you.

Chapter 19

Adopting XP

Adopt XP one practice at a time, always addressing the most pressing problem for your team. Once that's no longer your most pressing problem, go on to the next problem.

Thanks to Don Wells for the simple, obviously correct answer to the question of how to adopt XP.

1. Pick your worst problem.
2. Solve it the XP way.
3. When it's no longer your worst problem, repeat.

The two obvious places to start are testing and the Planning Game. Many projects are plagued with quality problems, or with an imbalance of power between business and development. The second XP book, *Extreme Programming Applied: Playing to Win* (projected publication in winter 2000), will address these two topics because they are such common places to start.

There are many advantages to this approach. It's so simple even I could understand it (once Don smacked me with it). Because you are only learning one practice at a time, you can do a thorough job of learning each one. Because you are always addressing your most pressing problem, you have plenty of motivation to change, and you get immediate positive feedback for your efforts.

Solving the most pressing problem also addresses the objection to XP that it is "one size fits all." In adopting each practice, you will shape it to your situation. If you don't have a problem, you won't even consider solving it the XP way.

Don't underestimate the importance of the physical environment when adopting XP, even if you aren't aware of it as a problem. I often start with a screwdriver and an Allen wrench. I'll add two more steps to the process.

-1. Rearrange the furniture so you can pair program and the customer can sit with you.

 0. Buy some snack food.

Chapter 20

Retrofitting XP

Projects that want to change their existing culture are far more common than projects that can create a new culture from scratch. Adopt XP on running projects a little at a time, starting with testing or planning.

Adopting XP with a new team is a challenge. Adopting it with an existing team and existing code base is even harder. You have all the existing challenges—learning the skills, coaching, making the process your own. You also have the immediate pressure of keeping production software running. The software is unlikely to be written to your new standards. It is likely to be more complex than it needs to be. It is unlikely to be tested to the degree you would like. On a new team, you can select only those people who are willing to try XP. An existing team is likely to have some skeptics. And on top of that, all the desks are already set up and you can't even pair program.

You will have to take more time to retrofit XP on a project than you would to adopt on the equivalent new team. That's the bad news. The good news is that there are some risks that a "green field" XP development has to face that you won't have to face. You will never be in the risky position of thinking you have a good idea for software but not really knowing. You will never be in the risky position of making lots of decisions without the immediate and brutal feedback you get from real customers.

I talk to lots of teams that say, "Oh yes, we are already doing XP. Everything but that testing stuff. And we have a 200-page requirements document. But everything else is exactly how we do it." That's why this chapter is set up practice by practice. If you are already doing the same practice advocated by XP, you can ignore that subsection. If there is some new practice that you want to pick up, check out the subsection devoted to that practice.

How can you adopt XP with an existing team on software that is already in production? You will have to modify the adoption strategy in the following areas:

- Testing
- Design
- Planning
- Management
- Development

Testing

Testing is perhaps the most frustrating area when you are shifting existing code to XP. The code written before you have tests is scary. You never know quite where you stand. Will this change be safe? You're not sure.

As soon as you start writing the tests, the picture changes. You have confidence in the new code. You don't mind making changes. In fact, it's kind of fun.

Shifting between old code and new code is like night and day. You will find yourself avoiding the old code. You have to resist this tendency. The only way to gain control in this situation is to bring all the code forward. Otherwise ugly things will grow in the dark. You will have risks of unknown magnitude.

In this situation, it is tempting to try to just go back and write the tests for all the existing code. Don't do this. Instead, write the tests on demand.

- When you need to add functionality to untested code, write tests for its current functionality first.
- When you need to fix a bug, write a test first.
- When you need to refactor, write tests first.

What you will find is that development feels slow at first. You will spend much more time writing tests than you do in normal XP, and you will feel like you make progress on new functionality more slowly than before. However, the parts of the system that you visit all the time, the parts that attract attention and new features, will quickly be thoroughly tested. Soon, the parts of the system that are used most will feel like they were written with XP.

Design

Transitioning to XP design is much like transitioning to XP testing. You will notice that the new code feels completely different than the old code. You will want to fix everything at once. Don't. Take it a bit at a time. As you add new functionality, be prepared to refactor first. You are always prepared to refactor first before implementing in XP development, but you will have to do it more often as you are transitioning to XP.

Early on in the process, have the team identify some large-scale refactoring goals. There may be a particularly tangled inheritance hierarchy, or a piece of functionality scattered across the system that you want to unify. Set these goals, put them on cards, and display them prominently. When you can say the big refactoring is done (it may take months or even a year of nibbling), have a big party. Ceremoniously burn the card. Eat and drink well.

The effect of this strategy is much like the effect of the demand-driven testing strategy. Those parts of the system that you visit all the time in your development activities will soon feel just like the code that you are writing now. The overhead of extra refactorings will soon fade.

Planning

You will have to convert your existing requirements information to story cards. You will have to educate your customer about the rules of the game. The customer will have to decide what constitutes the next release.

The biggest challenge (and opportunity) of switching to XP planning is teaching your customer how much more they can get from the team. They probably haven't had the experience of a development team that welcomes requirements changes. It takes awhile to get used to how much more the customer can get from the team.

Management

One of the most difficult transitions is getting used to XP management. XP management is a game of indirection and influence. If you are a manager, you will probably catch yourself making decisions that should be made by programmers or customers. If you do, don't panic. Just remind yourself and everyone else present that you are learning. And then ask the right person to make the decision and let you know what they decided.

Programmers suddenly confronted with new responsibilities are unlikely to do a great job immediately. As a manager, you must be careful during the transition period to remind everyone of the rules they have chosen. Under pressure, everyone will revert to previous patterns of behavior, whether these patterns worked or not.

The feeling will be a little like transitioning the design or the tests. At first, it will feel awkward. You will know that you aren't going at full speed. As you pay attention to the situations that occur day in and day out, you (and the programmers and the customers) will learn how to handle them smoothly. You will quickly begin feeling comfortable with your new process. From time to time, however, a situation will arise that you haven't "done extreme" before. When this happens, take a step back. Remind the team of the rules, values, and principles. Then decide what to do.

One of the most difficult aspects of managing a galloping shift to XP is deciding that a team member isn't working out. In this situation, you are always better off without them. And you should make the change as soon as you are sure the situation isn't going to get any better.

Development

The first thing you have to do is get those desks set up right. No kidding. Reread the material about pair programming (Chapter 16, Development Strategy). Set up your desks so two people can sit side by side and shift the keyboard back and forth without having to move their chairs.

On the one hand, when you are transitioning to XP you should be more rigid about pair programming than you would normally have to be. Pair programming may be uncomfortable at first. Force yourself to do it, even if you don't feel like it. On the other hand, take a break sometime. Go off by yourself and code for a couple of hours. Throw away the results, of course, but don't destroy your joy in programming just to be able to say you paired for 30 hours in one week.

Nibble away at the testing and design problems. Bring all the code you touch up to your agreed-on coding standards. You will be surprised how much you can learn from even this simple activity.

In Trouble?

Some of you reading this will have an existing team but your software isn't yet in production. Your project may be in a lot of trouble. XP may look like a possible salvation.

Don't count on it. If you had used XP from the beginning, you might (or might not) have avoided your current situation. However, if switching horses midstream is tough, switching from a drowning horse is ten times as tough. Emotions are going to be high. Morale is going to be low.

If the choice is switch to XP or be fired, first realize that your chances of consistently adopting new practices aren't very good. Under stress, you revert to old habits. You already have lots of stress. Your chances of successfully making the switch are drastically reduced. Make a more modest goal for yourself than saving the whole project. Take it one day at a time. Celebrate how much you can learn about testing, or managing indirectly, or how beautiful you can make a design, or how much code you can delete. Perhaps enough order will emerge from the chaos that you won't mind coming in the next day.

However, if you're going to switch a troubled project to XP, make it a dramatic gesture. Half measures are going to leave everybody in more or less the same state that they were before. Carefully evaluate the current code base. Would you be better off without it? If so, flush it. All of it. Have a big bonfire and burn the old tapes. Take a week off. Start over fresh.

Chapter 21

Lifecycle of an Ideal XP Project

The ideal XP project goes through a short initial development phase, followed by years of simultaneous production support and refinement, and finally graceful retirement when the project no longer makes sense.

This chapter gives you an idea of the overall story of an XP project. It is idealized—you may have gotten the idea by now that no two XP projects could (or should) ever be exactly alike. What I hope you will get from this chapter is an idea of the overall flow of a project.

Exploration

Preproduction is an unnatural state for a system and should be gotten out of the way as quickly as possible. What was the phrase I heard recently? "To go into production is to die." XP says exactly the opposite. Not to be in production is to be spending money without making money. Now, it may just be my wallet, but I find the outgo/no income state to be very uncomfortable.

Before you can go into production, however, you have to believe that you can go into production. You have to have enough confidence in your tools that you believe you can get the program finished. You have to believe that once the code is done, you can run it day in and day out. You have to believe that you have (or can learn) the skills you need. The team members need to learn to trust each other.

The exploration phase is where all of this comes together. You are done with exploration when the customer is confident that there is more than enough material on the story cards to make a good first release and the programmers are confident that they can't estimate any better without actually implementing the system.

During exploration the programmers are using every piece of technology they are going to be using in the production system. They are actively exploring possibilities for the system architecture. They do this by spending a week or two building a system like what they will build eventually, but doing it three or four ways. Different pairs can try the system different ways and compare, or you could have two pairs try the system the same way and see what differences emerge.

If a week won't suffice to get a particular piece of technology up and running, then I would have to classify that technology as a risk. It doesn't mean that you shouldn't use it. But you should explore it more carefully and consider alternatives.

You might want to consider bringing in technology specialists during exploration so that your experiments aren't hampered by stupid little things that could be handled easily by someone who already has been there. Be wary about blindly accepting advice for the eventual use of the technology, however. Experts sometimes develop habits that are based on value systems not entirely in tune with extreme programming. The team will have to be comfortable with the practices they choose. Saying "The expert said so" isn't very satisfying when the project is spiraling out of control.

The programmers should also experiment with the performance limits of the technology they are going to use. If at all possible, they should simulate realistic loads with the production hardware and network. You don't have to have the whole system done to write a load simulator. You can get a lot of mileage by just calculating, for example, how many bytes per second your network will have to support and then running an experiment to see if it can provide the necessary bandwidth.

The programmers should also experiment with architectural ideas—how do you build a system for multiple levels of undo? Implement it three different ways for a day and see which one feels best. These little architectural explorations are most important when you find the user coming up with stories that you have no idea how to implement.

The programmers should estimate every programming task they embark on during exploration. When a task is done, they should report on the actual calendar time required for the task. Estimation practice will raise the team's confidence in their estimates when the time comes to make a public commitment.

While the team is practicing with the technology, the customer is practicing writing stories. Don't expect this to go completely smoothly. The stories at first won't be what you need. The key is getting the customers lots of quick feedback with the first few stories so they can learn quickly to specify what the programmers need and not specify what the programmers don't need. The key question is "Can the programmers confidently estimate the effort required by the story?" Sometimes the story needs to be written differently; sometimes the programmers need to go off and experiment for a bit.

If you have a team that already knows their technology and each other, the exploration phase could be as short as a few weeks. With a team that is completely new to a technology or domain, you might have to spend a few months. If exploration took longer than this, I might look for a small but real project that they could complete easily to lend urgency to the process.

Planning

The purpose of the planning phase is for the customers and programmers to confidently agree on a date by which the smallest, most valuable set of stories will be done. See the Planning Game for a way to run this. If you prepare during exploration, planning (the production of the commitment schedule) should take a day or two.

The plan for the first release should be between two and six months long. Shorter than that and you probably won't be able to solve any significant business problems. (But if you can, great! See Tom Gilb's *Principles of Software Engineering Management* for ideas about how to shrink the first release.) Longer than a few months and there is too much risk.

Iterations to First Release

The commitment schedule is broken into one- to four-week iterations. Each iteration will produce a set of functional test cases for each of the stories scheduled for that iteration.

The first iteration puts the architecture in place. Pick stories for the first iteration that will force you to create "the whole system," even if it is in skeletal form.

Picking stories for subsequent iterations is entirely at the discretion of the customer. The question to ask is, "What is the most valuable thing for us to be working on in this iteration?"

While you are clicking through the iterations, you are looking for deviations from the plan. Is everything taking twice as long as you had thought? Half as long? Are the test cases getting done on time? Are you having fun?

When you detect deviations from the plan, then you need to change something. Maybe the plan needs to change—add or remove stories or change their scope. Maybe the process needs to change—you find better ways of working your technology, or better ways of working XP.

Ideally, at the end of every iteration, the customer will have completed the functional tests and they will all run. Make a little ceremony out of the end of each iteration—buy pizza, shoot off fireworks, have the customer sign the completed story cards. Hey, you have just shipped quality software on time. It may only be three weeks' worth, but it is still an accomplishment and it is worth celebrating.

At the end of the last iteration, you are ready to go into production.

Productionizing

The end game of a release ("productionizing") sees a tightening up of the feedback cycle. Instead of three-week iterations, you may go to one-week iterations. You may have a daily stand-up meeting so everybody knows what everybody else is working on.

Typically there will be some process for certifying the software is ready to go into production. Be prepared to implement new tests to prove your fitness for production. Parallel testing is often applied at this stage.

You may also need to tune the performance of the system during this phase. I haven't said much about performance tuning in this book. I believe very strongly in the motto, "Make it run, make it right, make it fast." Late in the game is the perfect time to tune, because you will have as much knowledge as possible embedded in the design of the system, you will have the most realistic possible estimates of the production load on the system, and you are likely to have the production hardware available.

During productionizing, you will slow down the pace at which you evolve the software. It isn't that software stops evolving, but rather that risk becomes more important in your evaluation of whether a change deserves to go into this release. However, be aware that the more experience you have with a system, the more insight you will have into how it should be designed. If you begin finding lots of ideas that you can't justify putting into the system for this release, make a visible list so everybody can see where you will be going after this release goes into production.

When the software actually goes into production, throw a big party. Many projects never go into production. Having yours go live is a reason to celebrate. If you're not a little scared at the same time, you're crazy, but the party can help you blow off a little of the excess tension that is bound to have built up.

Maintenance

Maintenance is really the normal state of an XP project. You have to simultaneously produce new functionality, keep the existing system running, incorporate new people into the team, and bid farewell to members who move on.

Every release begins with an exploration phase. You may try big refactorings that you were afraid of late in the previous release. You may try new technology that you intend to add in the next release, or migrate to newer versions of the technology you are already using. You may experiment with new architectural ideas. The customer may try writing wacky new stories in search of a big winner for the business.

Developing a system that is in production is not at all the same as developing a system that isn't yet in production. You are more careful of the changes you make. You have to be prepared to interrupt development to react to production problems. You have live data that you have to be careful to migrate as you change the design. If preproduction weren't so dangerous, you'd keep from going into production forever.

Being in production is likely to change your development velocity. Be conservative with your new estimates. While you are exploring, measure the effect production support has on your development activities. I have seen an increase in the ratio of ideal engineering time to calendar time of 50% after having gone into production (from two calendar days per engineering day to three). Don't guess, though; measure.

Be prepared to change the team structure to deal with production. You may want to take turns manning the "help desk," so most of the programmers don't have to deal with production interruptions most of the time. Be careful to rotate all the programmers through the position—there are things you learn from supporting production that you just can't learn any other way. On the other hand, it isn't as much fun as developing.

Put newly developed software into production as you go along. You may know that parts of the software won't be executed. Put it into the production system anyway. I have been on projects where this cycle was daily or weekly, but in any case you shouldn't leave code lying around for longer than an iteration. The timing depends on how much verification and migration cost. The last thing you need when you are at the end of a release is to integrate a big gob of code, which "couldn't possibly" break anything. If you keep the production code base and the development code base nearly in sync, you will have much earlier warning of integration problems.

When new members come on the team give them two or three iterations where their job is to ask lots of questions, act as a pair programming partner, and read lots of tests and code. When they feel ready, they can take responsibility for a few programming tasks, but at a reduced load factor. When they have demonstrated that they can deliver, they can raise their load factor.

If the team changes gradually, in less than a year you can replace the original development team with all new people without disrupting either production support or ongoing development. This is a far less risky handoff than the typical "here it is and this stack of paper contains all the information you need." In fact, it is just as important to communicate the culture around the project as the details of the design and implementation, and that can only be done with personal contact.

Death

Dying well is as important as living well. This is as true for XP as for people.

If the customer can't come up with any new stories, then it is time to put the system into mothballs. Now is the time to write a five- to ten-page tour of the system, the kind of document you wish you would find when it comes time to change something in five years.

That's the good reason to die—the customer is happy with the system and can't think of anything they would like to add for the foreseeable future. (I've never experienced this, but I've heard about it, so I included it here.)

There is also a not-so-good reason to die—the system just isn't delivering. The customer needs features and you just can't add them economically. The defect rate creeps up to where it is intolerable.

This is the entropic death you have fought against for so long. XP is not magic. Entropy eventually catches XP projects, too. You just hope that it happens much later rather than sooner.

In any case, we have already posited the impossible—the system needs to die. It should happen with everybody's eyes open. The team should be aware of the economics of the situation. They, the customers, and the managers should be able to agree that the team, and the system, just can't deliver what is needed.

Then it is time for a fond farewell. Throw a party. Invite everyone who has worked on the system to come back and reminisce. Take the opportunity to try to plot the seeds of the system's downfall, so you'll know better what to look for in the future. Imagine with the team how they would run things differently next time.

Chapter 22

Roles for People

Certain roles have to be filled for an extreme team to work—
programmer, customer, coach, tracker.

A sports team works best when there are certain roles that someone
takes responsibility for. In soccer you have the goalie, the striker, the
sweeper, and so on. In basketball you have a point guard, a center, a
shooting guard, and so on.

A player taking one of these positions accepts a certain set of responsibilities—setting up teammates for scoring, preventing the other team
from scoring, perhaps managing a certain portion of the field. Some of
the roles are nearly solitary. Others require that the player correct the
mistakes of teammates, or manage their interactions.

These roles become customary, and sometimes even embedded in
the rules of the game, precisely because they work. At some time, probably every other combination of responsibilities has been tried. The
ones you see today are there because they worked and the other ones
didn't.

Good coaches are effective at getting a player to work well at their
position. They spot deviations from the usual practice of the position
and either help the player correct the deviation, or understand why it is
acceptable for that player to do things a little differently.

However, the great coach knows that the positions are merely customary, not laws of nature. From time to time, the game changes or
the players change enough so that a new position becomes possible or
an old one becomes obsolete. Great coaches are always looking for

what advantages could be had by creating new positions and eliminating existing ones.

Another facility of great sports coaches is their ability to mold the system to their players, instead of the other way around. If you have a system that works fabulously if you have quick players, and the team that shows up at the first workout is big and strong instead, then you will do better creating a new system that lets the team's talents shine. Lots of coaches can't do this. Instead, they get so focused on the beauty of "the system" that they can't see that it isn't working.

All of this is leading up to a big warning about what follows. Here are some roles that are found to have worked well on previous projects. If you have people who don't fit the roles, change the roles. Don't try to change the people (well, not too much). Don't act like there isn't a problem. If a role says, "This person must be willing to take large chances," and you have a watchmaker instead, you have to find a different division of the responsibilities that will meet your goals without the role in question being filled by a risk taker.

For example, I was talking to a manager about a team of his. A programmer was also the customer. I said that couldn't possibly work, since the programmer has to execute the process and make technical decisions and be sure to defer business decisions to the customer (see the Planning Game).

The manager argued with me. "This guy is a real bond trader," he said, "he just happens to know how to program, too. The other bond traders all like and respect him, and they are willing to trust him and confide in him. He has a solid vision for where the system is headed. The other programmers separate when he is speaking as the customer and when he is making technical decisions."

Okay. The rules here say that a programmer can't be the customer. In this case, the rules don't apply. What still applies is the separation of technical and business decisions. The whole team, the programmer/customer, and especially the coach, must be aware of which hat the programmer/customer is wearing at any given time. And the coach needs to be aware that no matter how well the arrangement has worked in the past, if they run into trouble, the dual role is a likely cause of problems.

Programmer

The programmer is the heart of XP. Actually, if programmers could always make decisions that carefully balanced short-term and long-term priorities, there would be no need for any other technical people on the project besides programmers. Of course, if the customer didn't absolutely need software to keep the business running, there would be no need for the programmers, so it won't do to get too big-headed about being the vital programmer.

On the surface, being an XP programmer looks a lot like being a programmer within other software development disciplines. You spend your time working with programs, making them bigger, simpler, faster. Beneath the surface, however, the focus is quite different. Your job isn't over when the computer understands what to do. Your first value is communication with other people. If the program runs, but there is some vital component of communication left to be done, you aren't done. You write tests that demonstrate some vital aspect of the software. You break the program into more smaller pieces, or merge pieces that are too small into larger, more coherent pieces. You find a system of names that more accurately reflects your intent.

This may sound like a high-minded pursuit of perfection. It is anything but. You try to develop the most valuable software for the customer, but not to develop anything that isn't valuable. If you can reduce the size of the problem enough, then you can afford to be careful with the work you do on what remains. Then, you are careful by habit.

There are skills that you must possess as an XP programmer that are not needed or at least not emphasized in other styles of development. Pair programming is a learnable skill, but one often at odds with the tendencies of the sort of people who typically get into programming. Perhaps I should state this less equivocally—nerds aren't generally good at talking. Now, there are certainly exceptions to this, and it is possible to learn to talk with other folks, but the fact is that you will have to communicate and coordinate closely with other programmers in order to be successful.

Another skill needed by the extreme programmer is the habit of simplicity. When the customer says, "You must do this and this and this," you have to be prepared to discuss which of those items is really necessary and how much of each. Simplicity also extends to the code you write. A programmer with every last analysis and design pattern ready at hand will not be likely to succeed with XP. Of course, you can do a better job if you have more tools in your toolbox than if you have fewer, but it is much more important to have a handful of tools that you know when not to use, than to know everything about everything and risk using too much solution.

You will need skills that are more technically oriented as well. You have to be able to program reasonably well. You have to be able to refactor, which is a skill with at least as much depth and subtlety as programming in the first place. You have to be able to unit test your code, which, like refactoring, requires taste and judgment to apply well.

You have to be willing to set aside the feeling of individual ownership of some portion of the system in favor of shared ownership of the whole system. If someone changes code that you wrote, in whatever part of the system, you have to trust the changes and learn from them. Of course, if the changes are wrong-headed, you are responsible for making things better.

Above all, you must be prepared to acknowledge your fears. Everybody is afraid—

- ⬦ Afraid of looking dumb
- ⬦ Afraid of being thought useless
- ⬦ Afraid of growing obsolete
- ⬦ Afraid of not being good enough

Without courage, XP just simply doesn't work. You would spend all of your time trying desperately not to fail. Instead, if you are willing, with the help of your team, acknowledge your fears. Then you can get on with the business of belonging to a team having fun writing great software.

Customer

The customer is the other half of the essential duality of extreme programming. The programmer knows how to program. The customer knows what to program. Well, not at first, of course, but the customer is willing to learn just as much as the programmer is.

Being an XP customer is not easy. There are skills you have to learn, like writing good stories, and an attitude that will make you successful. Most of all, though, you have to become comfortable influencing a project without being able to control it. Forces outside your control will shape what actually gets built just as much as the decisions you make. Changes in business conditions, technology, the composition and capability of the team, all of these have a huge impact on what software gets delivered.

You will have to make decisions. This is the hardest skill for some of the customers I have worked with. They are used to IT not delivering half of what they promised, and for what is delivered to be half-wrong. They have learned never to give an inch to IT, since they are bound to be disappointed anyway. XP won't work with such a customer. If you are an XP customer, the team needs you to say with confidence, "This is more important than that," "This much of this story is enough," "These stories together are just enough." And when times get tough, and they always get tough, the team needs you to be able to change your mind. "Well, I guess we don't absolutely have to have this until next quarter." Being able to make decisions like this will at times save your team, and reduce their stress enough so that they can do their best for you.

The best customers are those who will actually use the system being developed, but who also have a certain perspective on the problem to be solved. If you are one of these customers, you will have to be aware of when you are thinking a certain way because that is how things have always been done, rather than because of some essential quality in the problem. If you are a step or two removed from actually using the system, you will have to work extra hard to be sure that you accurately represent the needs of the real users.

You will have to learn how to write stories. This may seem like an impossible task at first, but the team will give you the gift of copious feedback on the first few you write, and you will rapidly learn how much ground to cover in each story, and what information to include and exclude.

You will have to learn to write functional tests. If you are the customer for an application with a mathematical basis, you will have an easier job—a few minutes or hours with a spreadsheet will suffice to create the data for a test case. Or perhaps your team will build you a tool to make entering new test cases easy. Programs with a formulaic basis (like workflow, for example), also need functional tests. You will have to work closely with the team to learn what kind of things it is helpful to test, and what kind of tests are redundant. Some teams may even assign you technical help for choosing, writing, and running the tests. Your goal is to write tests that let you say, "Well, if these run, then I'm confident the system will run."

Finally, you will have to demonstrate courage. There is a way from where you are today to where you want to be. This team can help you find it, if you will help them find it.

Tester

Since a lot of testing responsibility lies on the shoulders of the programmers, the role of tester in an XP team is really focused on the customer. You are responsible for helping the customer choose and write functional tests. If the functional tests aren't part of the integration suite, you are responsible for running the functional tests regularly and posting the results in a prominent place.

An XP tester is not a separate person, dedicated to breaking the system and humiliating the programmers. However, someone has to run all tests regularly (if you can't run your unit and functional tests together), broadcast test results, and to make sure that the testing tools run well.

Tracker

As a tracker, you are the conscience of the team (think Jiminy Cricket, but with better clothes).

Doing good estimates is a matter of practice and feedback. You have to make lots of estimates, and then notice how reality conformed to your guesses. Your job is to close the loop on feedback. The next time the team is making estimates, you need to be able to say, "Two thirds of our estimates last time were at least 50% too high." On an individual basis, you need to be able to say, "Your task estimates are either way too high or way too low." The next estimates to come out are still the responsibility of the people who have to implement whatever is being estimated, but you have given them the feedback so that when they come out, they can be better than last time.

You are also responsible for keeping an eye on the big picture. Halfway through an iteration you should be able to tell the team whether they are going to make it if they follow the current course or if they need to change something. A couple of iterations into a commitment schedule you should be able to tell the team whether they are going to make the next release without making big changes.

You are the team historian. You keep a log of functional test scores. You keep a log of defects reported, who accepted responsibility for each, and what test cases were added on each defect's behalf.

The skill you need to cultivate most is the ability to collect the information you need without disturbing the whole process more than necessary. You want to disturb the process a little, to keep people aware of how much time they actually spent on a task in a way they might not be aware of if you didn't ask. But you can't be such a pain in the neck that people avoid answering you.

Coach

As coach, you are responsible for the process as a whole. You notice when people are deviating from the team's process and bring this to the team's attention. You remain calm when everyone else is panicking, remembering that in the next two weeks you can only get two weeks' worth of work done or less, and either two weeks' worth is enough or it isn't.

Everyone on an XP team is responsible for understanding their application of XP to some extent. You are responsible for understanding it much more deeply—what alternative practices might help the current set of problems; how other teams are using XP; what the ideas behind XP are; and how they relate to the current situation.

The most difficult thing I have found about being a coach is that you work best when you work indirectly. If you see a mistake in the design, first you have to decide whether it is important enough that you should intervene at all. Every time you guide the team, you make them that much less self-reliant. Too much steering and they lose the ability to work without you, resulting in lowered productivity, lowered quality, and lowered morale. So, first you have to decide whether the problem you see is enough of a problem that you need to accept the risk of intervening.

If you decide you really do know better than the team, then you have to make your point as unobtrusively as possible. For example, it is far better to suggest a test case that can only be implemented cleanly by fixing the design, than it is to just go and fix the design yourself. But it is a skill to not directly say what you see, but to say it in such a way that the team sees it, too.

Sometimes, however, you must be direct, direct to the point of rudeness. Confident, aggressive programmers are valuable precisely because they are confident and aggressive. However, this leaves them vulnerable to a certain kind of blindness, and the only cure is plain speaking. When you have let a situation deteriorate to the point that the gentle hand on the yoke can no longer work, you have to be prepared to grab the yoke with both hands and steer. But only long enough to get the team back on track. Then you have to let one hand drop again.

I want to say something here about skills coaching. I am always in the position of teaching the skills of XP—simple design, refactoring, testing. But I don't think this is necessarily part of the job description of coach. If you had a team that was technically self-sufficient, but needed help with their process, you could coach without being a techno-whiz. You would still have to convince the propeller-heads that they should listen to you. But once the skills are there, my job is mostly reminding the team of the way they said they wanted to act in various situations.

The role of coach diminishes as the team matures. In keeping with the principles of distributed control and accepted responsibility, "the process" should be everybody's responsibility. Early in the shift to XP this is too much to ask any programmer.

Consultant

XP projects don't spawn a lot of specialists. Since everyone is pairing with everyone else, and the pairs float around so much, and anyone can accept responsibility for a task if they want to, there is little chance that dark holes will develop where only one or two people understand the system.

This is a strength, because the team is extremely flexible, but it is also a weakness, because from time to time the team needs deep technical knowledge. The emphasis on simplicity of design reduces the occurrence of the need for the pointy hat, but it will happen from time to time.

When it does, the team needs a consultant. Chances are, if you are a consultant you won't be used to working extreme. You are likely to view what the team does with a certain amount of skepticism. But the team should be extremely clear about the problem they need to solve. They will be able to provide you with tests to show exactly when it has been solved (in fact they will insist on the tests).

What they won't do is let you go off and solve the problem by yourself. If the team needs deep technical knowledge in an area once, they are likely to need it again. Their goal is to get you to teach them how to solve their own problem. So, one or two team members will sit with you as you solve the problem. They will likely ask you lots of questions. They will challenge your design and assumptions, to see if they can't find something simpler that will still work.

And when you are done, they will most likely throw away everything you have done and do it over themselves. Don't be insulted. Every day they do this to themselves a little bit, and probably once a month they throw away a day's work.

Big Boss

If you're the big boss, what the team needs most from you is courage, confidence, and occasional insistence that they do what they say they do. It is likely to be difficult for you to work with the team at first. They are going to ask you to check up on them frequently. They are going to explain the consequences of changes in the situation. For example, if you don't get them the new tester they asked for, they will explain exactly what they think that will do to the schedule. If you don't like their answer, they will invite you to reduce the scope of the project.

Coming from an XP team, this constitutes honest communication. They aren't whining, really they aren't. They want you to know as soon as possible when things are differing from the plan, so you have as much time to react as possible.

The team needs you to have courage, because what they do will sometimes seem crazy, especially if you have a background in software development. Some of the ideas you will recognize and approve of, like the strong emphasis on testing. Some don't seem to make sense at first, like pair programming being a more effective way to program and constantly refining the design being a lower-risk way to design. But watch and see what they produce. If it doesn't work, you can step in. If it does, you're golden, because you will have a team that is working productively, that keeps its customers happy, and that does everything they can to never surprise you.

This doesn't mean that the team won't screw up from time to time. They will. You will look at what they are doing, and it won't make sense to you, and you'll ask them to explain it, and the explanation won't make sense. That's when the team is relying on you to make them stop and take a look at what they are doing. You got to your position for a reason. The team wants to put that skill to work for them when they need it. And, frankly, to keep it out of the way when they don't need it.

Chapter 23

20–80 Rule

The full value of XP will not come until all the practices are in place. Many of the practices can be adopted piecemeal, but their effects will be multiplied when they are in place together.

Software programmers are used to dealing with the 20–80 rule—80% of the benefit comes from 20% of the work. XP makes use of this rule itself—put the most valuable 20% of functionality into production, do the most valuable 20% of the design, rely on the 20–80 rule to defer optimization.

For the 20–80 rule to apply, the system in question must have controls that are relatively independent of each other. For example, when I tune the performance of a program, each possible place I could tune generally has little effect on the other places I could tune. I never find myself in a situation where I tune the biggest time hog, only to find that because of that tuning I can't tune the next one. In a system with independent controls, some of them are bound to be more important than others.

Ward Cunningham tells of a book that got him onto advanced ski slopes called *The Athletic Skier.*[1] Half the book is about tuning your boots, getting them set up just right so you can feel the mountain and be on balance. And then the book says, "but you will only see 20% of the improvement when you have done 80% of these exercises." It goes on to explain that there is a huge difference between being on balance

---

1. Warren Witherell and Doug Evrard, *The Athletic Skier*, Johnson Books, 1993.

and being off balance. If you are a little off balance, you may as well be a lot off balance. And it is a host of little factors, like getting your boots just right, that allow you to be right on balance. If any one is off, you'll be off. You will see slow improvement all along, but the last few changes you make will dramatically improve your skiing.

I think (and this is just a hypothesis) that XP is like that. The practices and the principles work together with each other to create a synergy that is greater than the sum of the parts. It's not just that you do testing, it's that you are testing a simple system, and it got simple because you had a pair programming partner who challenged you to refactor and reminded you to write more tests and patted you on the back when you got rid of complexity and ....

This poses a dilemma. Is XP all or nothing? Do you have to follow these practices to the letter or risk not seeing any improvement? Not at all. You can get significant gains from parts of XP. It's just that I believe there is much more to be gained when you put all the pieces in place.

Chapter 24

What Makes XP Hard

Even though the individual practices can be executed by blue-collar programmers, putting all the pieces together and keeping them together is hard. It is primarily emotions—especially fear—that make XP hard.

When people hear me talk about XP they say, "But you make it sound so simple." Well, that's because it is simple. It doesn't take a Ph.D. in computer science to contribute to an XP project (in fact, the Ph.D.'s sometimes have the most trouble).

XP is simple in its details, but it is hard to execute.

Let's run that again. XP is simple, but it isn't easy? Exactly. The practices that make up XP can be learned by anyone who has convinced someone else to pay them to program. That isn't the hard part. The hard part is putting all the pieces together, and then keeping them in balance. The pieces tend to support each other, but there are many problems, concerns, fears, events, and mistakes that can throw the process off balance. The whole reason you would "sacrifice" a senior technical person to be coach is because the problem of keeping the process on balance is so difficult.

I don't want to frighten you. Not more than necessary. Most software development groups could execute XP. (For exceptions, see the next chapter.)

Here are some of the things I've found hard about XP, both when I am applying it for my own code and when I am coaching teams adopting it. I don't want you to go borrowing trouble, but when the transition to XP is going rough (and there will be days, I promise), you should know that you are not alone. You're having a hard time because what you are doing is hard.

It's hard to do simple things. It seems crazy, but sometimes it is easier to do something more complicated than to do something simple. This is particularly true when you have been successful doing the complicated thing in the past. Learning to see the world in the simplest possible terms is a skill and a challenge. The challenge is that you may have to change your value system. Instead of being impressed when someone (like you, for instance) gets something complicated to work, you have to learn to be dissatisfied with complexity, not to rest until you can't imagine anything simpler working.

It's hard to admit you don't know. This makes it a personal challenge to adopt XP, a discipline based on the premise that you can develop only as fast as you learn. And if you're learning, that means you didn't know before. It will be frightening to go to the customer and ask them to explain what are to them the most elementary concepts. It will be frightening to turn to your programming partner and admit that there are basic things about computer science that you frankly never quite got when you were in school. Or that you've forgotten.

It's hard to collaborate. Our whole education system is tuned to individual achievement. If you work with someone on a project, the teacher calls it cheating and punishes you. The reward systems in most companies, with individual evaluations and raises (often cast as a zero sum game), also encourages individual thinking. You will likely have to learn new people skills, interacting as closely with your team as you will in XP.

It's hard to break down emotional walls. The smooth running of an XP project relies on the smooth expression of emotions. If someone is getting frustrated or angry and not talking about it, it won't be long before the team starts to underperform. We have learned to separate our emotional lives and our business lives, but the team can't function effectively if communication is not kept flowing, fears acknowledged, anger discharged, joy shared.

If this makes XP sound like a Big Sur, touchy-feely, brandy-sipping, hot-tubbing experience, well, I don't think of it that way. I've tried to develop software pretending I didn't have any emotions and demanding distance from my coworkers. It didn't work. I talk about how I feel and I listen when others talk about how they feel, and the process goes much more smoothly.

The XP practices are so sideways to what we have heard and said and maybe even been successful with in the past. One of the big difficulties is just how contrary XP sounds. I'm often afraid when I first meet a new manager that I will sound radical or crazy or impractical. However, I don't know a better way to develop software, so I eventually get over it. Be prepared to have people react strongly when you explain XP, however.

Little problems can have huge effects. I think of the checks and balances of XP as being quite robust, the process able to tolerate lots of variation. However, small things can often make huge differences. Once on the Chrysler C3 payroll project the team was having trouble hitting their estimates. Iteration after iteration, a story or two would slip out. It took me three or four months to diagnose the problem. I heard someone talking about "First Tuesday Syndrome." I asked what that was and a team member replied, "The feeling you get the day after the iteration planning meeting when you come in, look at your stories, and realize you have no idea how to implement them in the estimated time."

I had originally specified the process as:

1. Sign up for tasks
2. Estimate your tasks
3. Rebalance if someone is overcommitted

The team had wanted to avoid the third step, so they changed the process to:

1. Estimate tasks collectively
2. Sign up for tasks

The problem was that the person who accepted responsibility for a task didn't own the estimate. They would come in the next day and say, "Why is this going to take three days? I don't even know what is involved." You may be able to guess that this isn't the most productive state for a programmer. People were losing a day or two to First Tuesday Syndrome every iteration. No wonder they weren't hitting their targets.

I tell this story to illustrate that small problems with the process can have large effects. I don't mean to say that you should do everything exactly as I say or you'll be sorry, buster. You still have to accept responsibility for your own process. But what makes XP hard is exactly this—by accepting responsibility for your own development process, you are accepting responsibility for being aware and fixing it when there is a problem.

Driving projects by steering a little at a time goes contrary to the car-pointing metaphor prevalent in lots of organizations. A final difficulty, and one that can easily sink an XP project, is that steering is just not acceptable in many company cultures. Early warning of problems is seen as a sign of weakness or complaining. You will need courage when your company asks you to act contrary to the process you have chosen for yourself.

Chapter 25

When You Shouldn't Try XP

The exact limits of XP aren't clear yet. But there are some abso-lute showstoppers that prevent XP from working—big teams, distrustful customers, technology that doesn't support graceful change.

There are practices in XP that are a good idea regardless of what you think about the whole picture. You should do them. Period. Testing is a good example. The Planning Game probably works, even if you spend more time on estimation and up-front design. However, as the 20–80 rule proposes, there is probably a huge difference between all of it and not all of it.

And all of XP, frankly, is not a story that can be told everywhere. XP is not a story that should be told everywhere. There are times and places and people and customers that would explode an XP project like a cheap balloon. And it is important not to use XP for those projects. It is as important not to use XP where it is bound to fail as it is important to use it where it provides real advantages. That's what this book is about—deciding when to use XP and when not to use XP.

That said, I won't be telling you "Don't use XP to build missile nosecones." I haven't ever built missile nosecone software, so I don't know what it is like. So I can't tell you that XP will work. But I also can't tell you that it won't work. If you write missile nosecone software, you can decide for yourself whether XP might or might not work.

I have failed with XP enough to know some of the ways it certainly doesn't work, however. Take this as a list of environments that I know don't do well with XP.

The biggest barrier to the success of an XP project is culture. Not national culture, although that has an effect, too, but business culture. Any business that runs projects by trying to point the car in the right direction is going to have a rough time with a team that insists on steering.

A variant of "pointing the car" is the big specification. If a customer or manager insists on a complete specification or analysis or design before they begin the small matter of programming, then there is bound to be friction between the team's culture and the customer or manager's culture. The project may still be able to be successful using XP, but it won't be easy. You will be asking the customer or manager to trade a document that gave them a feeling of control for a dialog (the Planning Game) that requires them to be continuously engaged. That can be scary to a person who is already overcommitted.

On the other hand, I worked with a bank customer that just loved big piles of paper. They insisted throughout the project that we would have to "document" the system. We kept telling them that of course, when the customer wanted to make the tradeoff to get less functionality and more paper, we would be glad to oblige. We heard about this "documentation" for months. As the project went forward, and it became clear just how valuable the tests were for keeping the system stable and for communicating the intended use of the objects, the pronouncements about documentation became quieter and quieter, although they were still there. In the end, what the development manager said he really wanted was a four-page introduction to the main objects in the system. As far as he was concerned, anyone who couldn't find the rest of what they needed to know from the code and the tests had no business touching the code.

Another culture that is not conducive to XP is one in which you are required to put in long hours to prove your "commitment to the company." You can't execute XP tired. If the amount produced by a team working at top speed isn't enough for your company, then XP isn't your solution. The second consecutive week of overtime on an XP project is a sure sign that something is wrong with the process, and you'd better fix what's wrong.

Really smart programmers sometimes have a hard time with XP. Sometimes the smart people have the hardest time trading the "Guess Right" game for close communication and continuous evolution.

Size clearly matters. You probably couldn't run an XP project with a hundred programmers. Nor fifty. Nor twenty, probably. Ten is definitely doable. With three or four programmers you can safely shed some of the practices that are focused on programmer coordination, like the Iteration Planning Game. The amount of functionality to be produced and the number of people producing it don't have any sort of simple linear relationship. If you have a big project, you might want to experiment with XP—try it for a month with a small team—to see how fast you might be able to develop.

The biggest bottleneck in scaling is the single-threaded integration process. You would have to expand this somehow to deal with more code streams than could easily be accommodated by a single integration machine.

You shouldn't use XP if you are using a technology with an inherently exponential cost curve. For example, if you are developing the Nth mainframe system to use the same relational database and you aren't absolutely sure the database schema is exactly what you need, now and forever, you shouldn't use XP. XP relies on keeping the code clean and simple. If you make the code complicated to avoid modifying 200 existing applications, pretty soon you will lose the flexibility that brought you to XP in the first place.

Another technology barrier to XP is an environment where a long time is needed to gain feedback. For example, if your system takes 24 hours to compile and link, you will have a hard time integrating, building, and testing several times a day. If you have to go through a two-month quality assurance cycle before you can put software in production, you will have trouble learning enough to be successful.

I've seen environments where it was simply impossible to realistically test software—you are in production on a million-dollar machine that is operating at capacity and there simply isn't another million dollars around. Or there are so many combinations of possible problems that you can't run any meaningful test suite in less than a day. In this case, you are absolutely right to trade testing for thought. But at that point you aren't doing XP any more. When I programmed in that sort of environment, I never felt free to evolve the design of the software; I had to build in flexibility up front. You can still build fine software this way, but you shouldn't be using XP to do it.

Remember the story of the senior people with the corner offices? If you have the wrong physical environment, XP can't work. One big room with little cubbies around the outside and powerful machines on tables in the middle is about the best environment I know. Ward Cunningham tells the story of the WyCash project where they had individual offices. However, the offices were big enough for two people to work in comfortably, so when folks wanted to pair, they would just go to one office or the other. If you absolutely can't move the desks, or the noise level prevents conversation, or you can't be close enough for serendipitous communication, you won't be able to execute XP at anything like its full potential.

What doesn't work for sure? If you have programmers on two floors, forget it. If you have programmers widely separated on one floor, forget it. Geographically separated—you could probably do this if you really had two teams working on related projects with limited interaction. I would start them out as one team, ship the first release, then split the team along the natural fracture lines of the application and grow each part.

Finally, there is absolutely no way you can do XP with a baby screaming in the room. Trust me on this one.

Chapter 26

XP at Work

XP can accommodate the common forms of contract, albeit with slight modifications. Fixed price/fixed scope contracts, in particular, become fixed price/fixed date/roughly fixed scope contracts when run with the Planning Game.

How can you fit XP to common business practices? The wrong form of contract can easily break a project, regardless of tools, technology, and talent.

This chapter examines some business arrangements for software development and how you might use them with XP.

Fixed Price

Folks seem to have the most trouble with running a fixed price contract extreme. How can you do a fixed price/fixed date/fixed scope contract if you play the Planning Game? You will end up with a fixed price/fixed date/roughly variable scope contract.

Every project I've worked on that had fixed price and scope ended with both parties saying, "The requirements weren't clear." And the typical fixed price and scope project pulls the two parties in exactly opposite directions. The supplier wants to do as little as possible and the customer wants to demand as much as possible. Within this tension, both parties want a successful project, so they back off of their primary goals, but the tension is always there.

Within XP, the relationship changes in a subtle but important way. The initial scope is a "for instance." "For example, for 5,000,000 deutsche marks we think we could produce the following stories in 12 months." The customer has to decide if those stories would be worth 5,000,000 DM. If those initial stories are what the team ends up producing, great. Chances are that the customer will replace some of the stories with even more valuable ones. Nobody complains if they get something more valuable. Everybody complains if they get what they asked for but it isn't what they now know that they want.

Instead of fixed price/date/scope, the XP team offers something more like a subscription. The team will work at top speed for the customer for a certain amount of time. They will track the customer's learning. At the beginning of every iteration the customer has a formal chance to change direction, to introduce entirely new stories.

Another difference XP introduces is caused by small releases. You would never do an XP project for 18 or even 12 months without being in production. Once the team has signed up to do 12 months' worth of stories, they will play the Planning Game with the customer to determine the scope of the first release. So a 12-month contract might put the system into production after three or four months, with monthly or bimonthly releases thereafter. Incremental delivery builds in the opportunity for the customer to terminate the contract if progress is slower than initially estimated, or if business conditions make the whole project nonsense, and it gives the customer natural points to change the direction of the project.

Outsourcing

In the typical outsourced development, the customer ends up with a pile of code that they don't know how to maintain. They have three choices.

- ✧ They can bring the further evolution of the system to a crawl by trying to do it themselves.
- ✧ They can hire the original supplier to continue evolving the system (but the original supplier can charge them a lot).
- ✧ They can hire another supplier who doesn't know the code well.

You could do this with XP if you really wanted. The team could come live with the customer or the customer could come live with the team. They would play the Planning Game to decide what to do. When the contract was done, the team could go away and leave the customer with the code.

In a way this could be better than the typical outsourcing agreement. The customer would have the unit and functional tests to make sure that any changes they made didn't break existing functionality. The customer would have someone looking over the shoulders of the programmers so they would have some idea of what was inside the system. And the customer would be able to steer development as they went along.

Insourcing

Perhaps you get the idea that I'm not thrilled with outsourcing. The "big thump" delivery of outsourcing violates the incremental change principle. There is a slight twist on outsourcing that XP can deliver. What if you gradually replaced the members of the team with technical folks from the customer? I call this "insourcing."

It has many of the advantages of outsourcing. For example, it lets the supplier give the customer the benefit of detailed technical knowledge. By gradually shifting responsibility for the system, insourcing doesn't give the customer the risk that they will inherit a program they can't sustain.

Let's look at a sample insourcing arrangement provided by the supplier of a 10-person team. The contract is for 12 months. Initial development lasts three months, followed by deliveries once a month for 9 months. The customer supplies one technical person for the initial development. Thereafter, every other month the customer brings in one new person, and the supplier takes off one person. At the end of the contract, half the team are customer employees, ready to support the program and continue development, albeit at a slower pace.

Development would certainly not go as fast with all the turnover on the team as compared to an outsourcing agreement where the supplier's team remains stable. But the reduction of risk may be worth it.

XP supports insourcing by having the team constantly measure their speed. As team members shift around, the team as a whole is bound to go faster and slower. By constantly measuring achieved productivity, the team can adjust how much they commit to get done in the iterations of the Planning Game. As experts leave and less experienced people replace them, the team can reestimate the remaining stories.

Time and Materials

In a time and materials contract, the XP team bills by the hour or day. The rest of the process works as described.

The problem with T&M is that it puts the goals of the supplier at odds with the goals of the customer. The supplier wants to put as many people on the project as long as possible to maximize revenue. And the supplier is tempted to have the team work overtime to get more revenue per month. The customer wants as much functionality done as possible in as short a time as possible with the fewest possible people.

A good relationship between supplier and customer can make T&M work, but the underlying tension will always exist.

Completion Bonus

An excellent way to align the interests of supplier and customer in fixed price or T&M is to provide a bonus for timely completion of the project. There is a sense in which this is a sucker bet for the XP team. The control given by the Planning Game makes it very likely that they will be able to collect.

The evil twin of the completion bonus is the late penalty. Again, the Planning Game gives the XP team an advantage when agreeing to a late penalty. The team can be quite sure that they will complete the system on time, so they are unlikely to have to pay.

One feature of both completion bonuses and penalty clauses to watch for when used with XP is that the Planning Game inevitably results in changes in the scope of the project. A customer who was really out to screw the supplier could conceivably say, "It's April first and you haven't done all the stories in the original contract. No bonus, and you'd better start paying." And they could say this even if the system was successfully in production.

In general, this won't be a problem. If it's Christmas and there are presents under the tree, the customer is unlikely to count to see if they are exactly the presents on the original letter to Santa, especially if the customer has made the substitutions themselves.

If you are afraid of a customer sticking to the letter of the original stories to avoid paying a bonus, don't sign up for one. I would be wary of signing *any* kind of contract with that kind of customer.

Early Termination

One of the features of XP is that the customer can see exactly what they are getting as they go along. What if they discover halfway through that the whole project no longer makes sense? It is worth money to the customer to be able to pull the plug early. Consider adding a clause that lets the customer stop the project and pay a pro-rata share of the total cost, perhaps with an additional payment to compensate the supplier for having to find a new contract on short notice.

Frameworks

How could you use XP to develop a framework? If one of the rules is that you delete any functionality that isn't currently in use, wouldn't you end up deleting the whole framework?

XP is not big on "up-front reuse." In an XP project you would never spend six months creating frameworks, and then start using them. Nor would you separate the "framework team" from the "application team." In XP we build applications. If, after a few years of constant refinement, some of the abstractions start looking generally useful, that's the time to begin thinking about how to make them more widely available.

If the purpose of the project was developing a framework for external use, you could still use XP. In the Planning Game, Business would be played by a programmer who had actually built the kind of applications the framework was supposed to support. Features of the framework would turn into stories.

Once the framework was deployed outside the team, you would have to take a more conservative approach to refactorings that changed visible interfaces. Deprecation, where you give customers a certain amount of warning of the impending demise of a feature, lets you continue evolving the interface of the framework at the cost of keeping two interfaces alive for a while.

Shrinkwrap Products

You can also use XP for shrinkwrap software. The role of Business in the Planning Game is played by the marketing department. They are the ones who identify what stories the market wants, how much of each story is needed, and what order the stories should be implemented.

Hiring an expert user of the software to be part of Business is also a possibility. For example, game companies hire expert game players to play test their software. Financial trading software companies hire traders. If you were building a typesetting program, you would be crazy not to have an expert typesetter as part of the team. And that would be exactly the person you would want deciding whether story A or story B should be deferred to the next release.

Chapter 27

Conclusion

All methodologies are based on fear. You try to set up habits that prevent your fears from becoming reality. XP is no different in this respect from any other methodology. The difference is in what fears are embedded in XP. To the degree that XP is my baby, XP reflects my fears. I am afraid of:

- Doing work that doesn't matter
- Having projects canceled because I didn't make enough technical progress
- Making business decisions badly
- Having business people make technical decisions badly for me
- Coming to the end of a career of building systems and realizing that I should have spent more time with my kids
- Doing work I'm not proud of

XP also reflects the things I'm not afraid of:

- Coding
- Changing my mind
- Proceeding without knowing everything about the future
- Relying on other people
- Changing the analysis and design of a running system
- Writing tests

I had to learn not to fear these things. It didn't come naturally, especially with so many voices crying that these were exactly the things I should be afraid of, the things I should work very hard to avoid.

Expectation

A young man went to a sword master. Sitting in the sun outside the master's hut, the master gave him his first lesson. "Here is your wooden practice sword. I may hit you at any moment with my wooden sword, and you must block me." *Whack!*

"Ouch!"

"I said, 'at any moment.'" *Whack!*

"Ouch!"

The student raised his sword and looked fiercely at the master.

"Oh, I won't hit you now. You're expecting it."

Over the next few days, the student collected a lovely batch of bruises. He tried to pay attention to everything around him. But every time his attention slipped, *Whack!*

The student couldn't eat in peace. He couldn't sleep. He grew paranoid, peeping carefully around corners and listening intently for every little sound. But every time his eyes drooped or he forgot to listen, *Whack!*

Soon he sat down and cried in frustration. "I just can't take it. I'm not cut out to be a swordsman. I'm going home." At that moment, without understanding exactly why, he drew his sword and whirled, blocking the master's stroke. The master said, "Now you are ready to learn."

We can drive ourselves crazy with expectation. But by preparing for every eventuality we can think of, we leave ourselves vulnerable to the eventualities we can't imagine.

There is another way. The team can be perfectly prepared at any moment to go in whatever direction the business or the system demands. By giving up explicit preparation for change, paradoxically they become entirely prepared for any change. They expect nothing. They can no longer be surprised.

Annotated Bibliography

The purpose of this section is to give you a chance to dig deeper into the aspects of XP that interest you.

Philosophy

Sue Bender, *Plain and Simple: A Woman's Journey to the Amish*, HarperCollins, 1989; ISBN 0062501860.

> More is not better. Less may not be better, either.

Leonard Coren, *Wabi-Sabi: For Artists, Designers, Poets, and Philosophers*, Stone Bridge Press, 1994; ISBN 1880656124.

> XP does not aim for some kind of transcendental perfection in its programs. Wabi-sabi is an aesthetic celebration of the rough and functional.

Richard Coyne, *Designing Information Technology in the Postmodern Age: From Method to Metaphor*, MIT Press, 1995; ISBN 0262032287.

> Discusses the differences between modernist and postmodernist thought, a theme that plays throughout XP. There is also an excellent discussion of the importance of metaphors.

Philip B. Crosby, *Quality Is Free: The Art of Making Quality Certain*, Mentor Books, 1992; ISBN 0451625854.

> Breaks out of the zero-sum model of the four variables—time, scope, cost, and quality. You can't get software out the door faster by lowering quality. Instead, you get software out the door faster by raising quality.

George Lakoff and Mark Johnson, *Philosophy in the Flesh: The Embodied Mind and Its Challenge to Western Thought*, Basic Books, 1998; ISBN 0465056733.

> More good discussion of metaphors and thinking. Also, the description of how metaphors blend together to form wholly new metaphors is like what is happening in software engineering thought. The old metaphors drawn from civil engineering, mathematics, and so on are slowly becoming a uniquely software engineering metaphor.

Bill Mollison and Rena Mia Slay, *Introduction to Permaculture*, Ten Speed Press, 1997; ISBN 0908228082.

> High-intensity use in the Western world has generally been associated with exploitation and exhaustion. Permaculture is a discipline of farming that aims for sustainable high-intensity use through the synergistic effects of simple practices. Of particular interest is the idea that most growth occurs at the interactions between areas. Permaculture maximizes interactions with spirals of interplantings and lakes with wildly irregular edges. XP maximizes interactions with on-site customers and pair programming.

Attitude

Christopher Alexander, *Notes on the Synthesis of Form*, Harvard University Press, 1970; ISBN 0674627512.

> Alexander started by thinking about design as decisions resolving conflicting constraints, leading to further decisions to resolve the remaining constraints.

Christopher Alexander, *The Timeless Way of Building*, Oxford University Press, 1979; ISBN 0195024028.

> The relationship described between designers/builders and the users of buildings is much the same as the relationship between the programmers and the customer.

Cynthia Heimel, *Sex Tips for Girls*, Simon & Schuster, 1983; ISBN 0671477250.

> Genuine enthusiasm is the ultimate technique. With it, everything else falls in place. Without it, forget it.

The Princess Bride, Rob Reiner, director, MGM/UA Studios, 1987.

> "We'll never make it out alive."
>
> "Nonsense. You're just saying that because no one ever has."

Field Marshal Irwin Rommel, *Attacks: Rommel*, Athena, 1979; ISBN 0960273603.

> Entertaining examples of proceeding under apparently hopeless circumstances.

Frank Thomas and Ollie Johnston, *Disney Animation: The Illusion of Life*, Hyperion, 1995; ISBN 0786860707.

> Describes how the team structure at Disney evolved over the years to deal with changing business and technology. There are also lots of good tips for user interface designers and some really cool pictures.

Emergent Processes

Christopher Alexander, Sara Ishikawa, and Murray Silverstein, *A Pattern Language*, Oxford University Press, 1977; ISBN 0195019199.

> An example of a system of rules intended to produce emergent properties. We can argue about whether the rules are successful or not, but the rules themselves make interesting reading. Also, an excellent if too-brief discussion of the design of workspaces.

James Gleick, *Chaos: Making a New Science*, Penguin USA, 1988; ISBN 0140092501.

> A gentle introduction to chaos theory.

Stuart Kauffman, *At Home in the Universe: The Search for Laws of Self-Organization and Complexity*, Oxford University Press, 1996; ISBN 0195111303.

> A slightly less gentle introduction to chaos theory.

Roger Lewin, *Complexity: Life at the Edge of Chaos*, Collier Books, 1994; ISBN 0020147953.

> Yet more chaos theory.

Margaret Wheatley, *Leadership and the New Science*, Berrett-Koehler Pub, 1994; ISBN 1881052443.

> Answers the question, "What if we took the theory of self-organizing systems as a metaphor for management?"

Systems

Gerald Weinberg, *Quality Software Management: Volume 1, Systems Thinking*, Dorset House, 1991; ISBN 0932633226.

> A system and notation for thinking about systems of interacting actions.

Norbert Weiner, *Cybernetics*, MIT Press, 1961; ISBN 1114239089.

> A much deeper, if more difficult, introduction to systems.

Warren Witherell and Doug Evrard, *The Athletic Skier*, Johnson Books, 1993; ISBN 1555661173.

> A system of interrelated rules for skiing. The source of the 20–80 rule.

People

Tom DeMarco and Timothy Lister, *Peopleware*, Dorset House, 1999; ISBN 0932633439.

> Following *The Psychology of Computer Programming*, this book expanded the practical dialog about programs as written by peo-

ple, and in particular as written by teams of people. This book was my source for the principle of "accepted responsibility."

Carlo d'Este, *Fatal Decision: Anzio and the Battle for Rome*, Harper-Collins, 1991; ISBN 006092148X.

> What happens when ego gets in the way of clear thinking.

Robert Kanigel, *The One Best Way: Frederick Winslow Taylor and the Enigma of Efficiency*, Penguin, 1999; ISBN 0140260803.

> A biography of Taylor that puts his work into a context that helps show the limits of his thinking.

Gary Klein, *Sources of Power*, MIT Press, 1999; ISBN 0262611465.

> A simple, readable text on how experienced people actually make decisions in difficult situations.

Thomas Kuhn, *The Structure of Scientific Revolutions*, University of Chicago Press, 1996; ISBN 0226458083.

> XP comes as a paradigm shift for some folks. Paradigm shifts have predictable effects. Here are some of them.

Scott McCloud, *Understanding Comics*, Harper Perennial, 1994; ISBN 006097625X.

> The last couple of chapters talk about why people write comics. This made me think about why I write programs. There is also good material about the connection between the craft of comics and the art of comics, with parallels to the craft of writing programs (testing, refactoring) and the art of writing programs. There is also good material for user-interface designers about communicating with the spaces between things, and packing information into small spaces without clutter.

Geoffrey A. Moore, *Crossing the Chasm: Marketing and Selling High-Tech Products to Mainstream Customers*, HarperBusiness, 1999; ISBN 0066620023.

> Paradigm shifts from a business perspective. Different people will be prepared to adopt XP at different stages of its evolution. Some of the barriers are predictable, and have simple strategies to address them.

Frederick Winslow Taylor, *The Principles of Scientific Management*, 2nd ed. Institute of Industrial Engineers, 1998 (1st ed. 1911); ISBN 0898061822.

> This is the book that spawned "Taylorism." Specialization and strict divide-and-conquer served to produce more cars cheaper. My experience is that these principles make no sense as strategies for software development, no business sense, and no human sense.

Barbara Tuchman, *Practicing History*, Ballantine Books, 1991; ISBN 0345303636.

> A thoughtful historian thinks about how she does history. Like *Understanding Comics*, this book is good for reflecting on why you do what you do.

Colin M. Turnbull, *The Forest People: A Study of the Pygmies of the Congo*, Simon & Schuster, 1961; ISBN 0671640992.

> A society with plentiful resources. My dream is that it is possible to create this feeling within a team.

———, *The Mountain People*, Simon & Schuster, 1972; ISBN 0671640984.

> A society with scarce resources. Aptly describes several projects I've been on. I don't ever want to live that way again.

Mary Walton and W. Edwards Deming, *The Deming Management Method*, Perigee, 1988; ISBN 0399550011.

> Deming explicitly addresses fear as a barrier to performance. Everyone focuses in on the statistical quality-control methods, but there is much here about human emotion and its effects.

Gerald Weinberg, *Quality Software Management: Volume 4, Congruent Action*, Dorset House, 1994; ISBN 0932633285.

> When you say one thing and do another, bad things happen. This book talks about how to be congruent yourself, how to recognize incongruence in others, and what to do about it.

———, *The Psychology of Computer Programming*, Dorset House, 1998; ISBN 0932633420.

> Programs are written by people. Amazing, isn't it? Amazing how many folks still don't get it ....

———, *The Secrets of Consulting*, Dorset House, 1986; ISBN 0932633013.

> Strategies for introducing change. Useful for coaches.

Project Management

Fred Brooks, *The Mythical Man-Month*, Addison-Wesley, 1995; ISBN 0201835959.

> Stories to get you thinking about the four variables. The anniversary edition also has an interesting dialog around the famous "No Silver Bullet" article.

Brad Cox and Andy Novobilski, *Object-Oriented Programming—An Evolutionary Approach*, Addison-Wesley, 1991; ISBN 0201548348.

> The origins of the electrical engineering paradigm of software development.

Ward Cunningham, "Episodes: A Pattern Language of Competitive Development," in *Pattern Languages of Program Design 2*, John Vlissides, ed., Addison-Wesley, 1996; ISBN 0201895277 (also http://c2.com/ppr/episodes.html).

> Many of the ideas in XP first found expression in Episodes.

Tom DeMarco, *Controlling Software Projects*, Yourdon Press, 1982; ISBN 0131717111.

> Excellent examples of creating and using feedback to measure software projects.

Tom Gilb, *Principles of Software Engineering Management*, Addison-Wesley, 1988; ISBN 0201192462.

> A strong case for evolutionary delivery—small releases, constant refactoring, intense dialog with the customer.

Ivar Jacobson, *Object-Oriented Software Engineering: A Case Driven Approach*, Addison-Wesley, 1992; ISBN 0201544350.

> My source for driving development from stories (use cases).

Ivar Jacobson, Grady Booch, James Rumbaugh, *The Unified Software Development Process*, Addison Wesley Longman, 1999; ISBN 0201571692.

> Philosophically, there is much I agree with in this book—short iterations, an emphasis on metaphor, and using stories to drive development.

Philip Metzger, *Managing a Programming Project*, Prentice-Hall, 1973; ISBN 0135507561.

> The earliest programming project management text I've been able to find. There are nuggets here, but the perspective is pure Taylorism. And out of 200 pages, he spends exactly two paragraphs on maintenance—the opposite of XP.

Jennifer Stapleton, *DSDM Dynamic Systems Development Method: The Method in Practice,* Addison-Wesley, 1997; ISBN 0201178893.

> DSDM is one perspective on bringing rapid application development under control without giving up its benefits.

Hirotaka Takeuchi and Ikujiro Nonaka, "The new product development game," *Harvard Business Review* [1986], 86116:137–146.

> A consensus-oriented approach to evolutionary delivery. There are interesting ideas here for scaling XP up to more programmers.

Jane Wood and Denise Silver, *Joint Application Development*, 2 ed, John Wiley and Sons, 1995; ISBN 0471042994.

> JAD facilitators and XP coaches share a common value system—facilitate without directing, give power to people who know best how to make a decision, and eventually fade away. JAD is focused on creating a requirements document that the developers and customers agree can and should be implemented.

Programming

Kent Beck, *Smalltalk Best Practice Patterns*, Prentice-Hall, 1996; ISBN 013476904X.

> Modesty forbids.

Kent Beck and Erich Gamma, "Test Infected: Programmers Love Writing Tests," in *Java Report,* July 1998, volume 3, number 7, pp. 37–50.

> Writing automated tests with JUnit, the Java version of the xUnit testing framework.

Jon Bentley, *Writing Efficient Programs*, Prentice-Hall, 1982; ISBN 013970251-2.

> Cures for the "it ain't gonna be fast enough" blues.

Edward Dijkstra, *A Discipline of Programming*, Prentice-Hall, 1976; ISBN 013215871X.

> Programming-as-mathematics. I was particularly inspired by the emphasis on the search for beauty through programming.

Martin Fowler, *Analysis Patterns*, Addison Wesley Longman, 1996; ISBN 0201895420.

> A common vocabulary for making analysis decisions. More difficult to absorb than the design patterns, but in many ways deeper, since analysis patterns connect to what is going on in the business.

Martin Fowler, ed., *Refactoring: Improving the Design of Existing Code*, Addison Wesley Longman, 1999; ISBN 0201485672.

> The reference for refactoring. Get it. Study it. Use it.

Erich Gamma, Richard Helms, Ralph Johnson, and John Vlissides, *Design Patterns: Elements of Reusable Object-Oriented Software*, Addison-Wesley, 1995; ISBN 0201633612.

> A common vocabulary for making design decisions.

Donald E. Knuth, *Literate Programming*, Stanford University, 1992; ISBN 0937073814.

> A communication-oriented programming method. Maintaining literate programs is a pain, violating the principle that we should travel light. Still, every programmer should write a literate program from time to time, just to remind them of how much there is to communicate.

Steve McConnell, *Code Complete: A Practical Handbook of Software Construction*, Microsoft Press, 1993; ISBN 1556154844.

> A study in how much care you can profitably put into coding.

Bertrand Meyer, *Object-Oriented Software Construction*, Prentice-Hall, 1997; ISBN 0136291554.

> Design by contract is an alternative or extension to unit testing.

Other

Barry Boehm, *Software Engineering Economics*, Prentice-Hall, 1981; ISBN 0138221227.

> The standard reference on thinking about how much software costs and why.

Larry Gonick and Mark Wheelis, *The Cartoon Guide to Genetics*, HarperPerennial Library, 1991; ISBN 0062730991.

> A demonstration of the power of drawings as a communication medium.

John Hull, *Options, Futures, and Other Derivatives*, Prentice-Hall, 1997; ISBN 0132643677.

> The standard reference on options pricing.

Edward Tufte, *The Visual Display of Quantitative Information*, Graphics Press, 1992; ISBN 096139210X.

> More techniques for communicating numerical information through pictures. Good for understanding how best to present graphs of metrics, for example. Plus, the book is beautifully published.

Glossary

Where possible, XP uses widely accepted vocabulary. Where there are concepts in XP that are significantly different from concepts elsewhere, we highlight the differences by using new words. Here are the most important words in the XP lexicon.

Automated test   A test case that runs without any human intervention. The test checks to make sure the system calculates the expected values.

Coach   A role on the team for someone who watches the process as a whole and calls the team's attention to impending problems or opportunities for improvement.

Commitment schedule   A release and a date. The commitment schedule is refined one iteration at a time, and modified through reestimation and recovery.

Customer   A role on the team for choosing what stories the system has to satisfy, what stories are needed first and what can be deferred, and for defining tests to verify the correct functioning of the stories.

Engineering task   One thing the programmer knows the system must do. Tasks must be estimable at between one to three ideal programming days. Most tasks will derive directly from stories.

Entropy   The tendency of a system to get buggier over time, and for changes to become much more expensive.

Exploration   The phase of development when the customer communicates generally what all the system could do.

Functional test   A test written from the perspective of the customer.

Ideal programming time   The measure of an estimation tactic where you ask yourself, "How long would this take without distractions and disasters?"

Iteration   A one- to four-week period. At the beginning, the customer chooses the stories to be implemented in the iteration. At the end the customer can run their functional tests to see if the iteration succeeded.

Iteration plan   A pile of stories and a pile of tasks. Programmers sign up for tasks and estimate them.

Load factor   The measured ratio between ideal programming time and the calendar. Typically between 2 and 4.

Manager   A role on the team for allocating resources.

Pair programming   A programming technique where two people program with one keyboard, one mouse, and one monitor. In XP the pairs typically change a couple of times a day.

Partner   The other person who is pair programming with you.

Planning Game   The XP planning process. Business gets to specify what the system needs to do. Development specifies how much each feature costs and what budget is available per day/week/month.

Production   The phase of development when the customer is actually making money with the system.

Programmer   A role on the team for someone who analyzes, designs, tests, programs, and integrates.

Recovery   A planning move where the customer preserves the completion date of a release by reducing the scope of the release in response to increased estimates or decreased team speed.

Reestimation   A planning move where the team reestimates all the stories remaining in the release.

Refactoring A change to the system that leaves its behavior unchanged, but enhances some nonfunctional quality—simplicity, flexibility, understandability, performance.

Release A pile of stories that together make business sense.

Story One thing the customer wants the system to do. Stories should be estimable at between one to five ideal programming weeks. Stories should be testable.

System metaphor A story that everyone—customers, programmers, and managers—can tell about how the system works.

Team speed The number of ideal programming weeks the team can produce in a given amount of time.

Test case An automated set of stimuli and responses for the system. Each test case should leave the system the way it found it, so tests can run independently of each other.

Tracker A role on the team for measuring progress with numbers.

Unit test A test written from the perspective of the programmer.

Index

Addison-Wesley Computer and Engineering Publishing Group

How to Interact with Us

1. Visit our Web site

http://www.awl.com/cseng

When you think you've read enough, there's always more content for you at Addison-Wesley's web site. Our web site contains a directory of complete product information including:

- Chapters
- Exclusive author interviews
- Links to authors' pages
- Tables of contents
- Source code

You can also discover what tradeshows and conferences Addison-Wesley will be attending, read what others are saying about our titles, and find out where and when you can meet our authors and have them sign your book.

2. Subscribe to Our Email Mailing Lists

Subscribe to our electronic mailing lists and be the first to know when new books are publishing. Here's how it works: Sign up for our electronic mailing at **http://www.awl.com/cseng/mailinglists.html**. Just select the subject areas that interest you and you will receive notification via email when we publish a book in that area.

3. Contact Us via Email

cepubprof@awl.com
Ask general questions about our books.
Sign up for our electronic mailing lists.
Submit corrections for our web site.

bexpress@awl.com
Request an Addison-Wesley catalog.
Get answers to questions regarding your order or our products.

innovations@awl.com
Request a current Innovations Newsletter.

webmaster@awl.com
Send comments about our web site.

mikeh@awl.com
Submit a book proposal.
Send errata for an Addison-Wesley book.

cepubpublicity@awl.com
Request a review copy for a member of the media interested in reviewing new Addison-Wesley titles.

We encourage you to patronize the many fine retailers who stock Addison-Wesley titles. Visit our online directory to find stores near you or visit our online store: **http://store.awl.com/** or call **800-824-7799**.

Addison Wesley Longman
Computer and Engineering Publishing Group
One Jacob Way, Reading, Massachusetts 01867 USA
TEL 781-944-3700 • FAX 781-942-3076